Pharmaceutical Research, Democracy and Conspiracy

Pharmaceutical Research, Democracy and Conspiracy

International Clinical Trials in Local Medical Institutions

EDISON BICUDO
Kings College, London, UK

Routledge
Taylor & Francis Group

LONDON AND NEW YORK

First published in paperback 2024

First published 2014 by Gower Publishing

Published 2016 by Routledge
4 Park Square, Milton Park, Abingdon, Oxon OX14 4RN

and by Routledge
605 Third Avenue, New York, NY 10158

Routledge is an imprint of the Taylor & Francis Group, an informa business

Gower Applied Business Research
Our programme provides leaders, practitioners, scholars and researchers with thought provoking, cutting edge books that combine conceptual insights, interdisciplinary rigour and practical relevance in key areas of business and management.

British Library Cataloguing in Publication Data
A catalogue record for this book is available from the British Library

Library of Congress Cataloging-in-Publication Data
Bicudo, Edison, author.
  Pharmaceutical research, democracy and conspiracy : international clinical trials in local medical institutions / by Edison Bicudo.
    pages cm
  Includes bibliographical references and index.
  ISBN 978-1-4724-2357-3 (hardback) -- ISBN 978-1-4724-2358-0 (ebook) -- ISBN 978-1-4724-2359-7 (epub) 1. Drugs--Testing--Government policy. 2. Clinical trials--Moral and ethical aspects. 3. Pharmaceutical industry--Moral and ethical aspects. I. Title.
  RM301.27.B53 2014
  338.4'76151--dc23

                                                                            2013042241

ISBN: 978-1-4724-2357-3 (hbk)
ISBN: 978-1-03-283709-3 (pbk)
ISBN: 978-1-315-60032-1 (ebk)

DOI: 10.4324/9781315600321

Contents

List of Figures

List of Tables

Acknowledgements

For the conduct of this study, I relied on the kind help from professors and doctors based in different universities and countries. I am very grateful to Brian Salter (King's College London, UK), Alex Faulkner (University of Sussex, UK), Clare Williams and Steven Wainwright (University of Brunel, UK), María Jesús Santesmases (Centro de Ciencias Humanas y Sociales, Spain), Ilana Lowy (Cermes 3, France), Fabio Contel, Mónica Arroyo and Ana Vianna (University of Sao Paulo, Brazil), Barbara Rimer and Louise Marie Winstanly (University of North Carolina at Chapel Hill, USA).

I would also like to thank Chloe Yu for the friendship and the encouragement she gave me.

Foreword

Brian Salter[1]

Innovation in the life sciences is driven by an interlinked set of global markets with many and various governance arrangement at national and transnational levels. Predominant among these markets are research funding, scientific labour, research materials, venture capital, patenting and, last but not least, the clinical labour provided by the subjects of clinical trials. As the emerging economies of the BRICS countries (Brazil, Russia, India, China and South Africa) have sought to position themselves as competitors in the global bioeconomy, so they have necessarily engaged with these global markets. But the markets, or perhaps more accurately those who currently dominate them, have also sought to engage with the BRICS – with a consequent interplay of interests and power, structures and values as a new political economy of clinical trials is brought into existence.

In this book Edison Bicudo takes the market of clinical trials and uses it as a vehicle to explore the dimensions of the interaction between the hegemonic power of the global pharmaceutical industry and the ambitions of the emerging economies, in particular those of Brazil and South Africa. In so doing, he is taking the social science field beyond its customary focus on the operation and ethics of the pharmaceutical industry and into the domain of the local politics that drive the formation of new forms of clinical trial governance. How does this political economy work? This is underexplored, if not unexplored, territory. He shows how the governance infrastructure at national, local and institutional levels is constructed through political negotiations designed to make the market work in the interests of both the demand side (the contract research organizations [CROs] servicing the pharmaceuticals) and the supply side (the

---

1   Professor Brian Salter is the Director of the Global Biopolitics Research Group in the Department of Political Economy at King's College London and joint author with Herbert Gottweis and Catherine Waldby of *The Global Politics of Stem Cell Science: Regenerative Medicine in Transition* (Palgrave, 2009).

institutions and physicians providing the patients for clinical trials). Profit, as always, is the key, and tracking its path through the governance infrastructure illuminates the fundamentals of this particular economy.

The author's approach is guided by his understanding of two organizing rationalities which, drawing on Habermas, he characterizes as the instrumental and the communicational rationalities. Both form part of the encounter within which the new market arrangements are being negotiated and shaped. The first acts to facilitate the ambitions of the global pharmaceuticals; the second to arrange the social and institutional conditions necessary to the efficient accommodation of the new clinical trials economy. As becomes evident, there is much to be done. Transition to the new regime for the harnessing of local clinical labour to the pharmaceutical enterprise requires change at the national, institutional and professional levels. Laws must be adjusted, protocols invented and disseminated, economic contracts negotiated, and physician–patient relationships reformulated. As the market forces of the clinical trials industry are progressively released through the agency of governance infrastructure, so the health care system is itself reappraised. Where does its primary duty lie: health care delivery or health technology innovation? What, exactly, are the interests of patients and how are they manifest? With such tensions becoming manifest, the exercise of power and mediation is continuous.

In charting this distinctive perspective on the evolution of the relationship between emerging economies and the global pharmaceutical industry, the author draws on much original material in addition to the customary sources of internet and documentary evidence. The 76 interviews he conducted in the UK, Spain, France, Brazil and South Africa span the full range of institutions and actors involved in the new clinical trials economy, including CROs, hospitals and research centres. Armed with this qualitative material, he is able to provide both empirical insights and theoretical illumination, using the platform of the Habermas approach to show the general and specific machinery of the governance construction that is required if the political economy of clinical trials is to serve the interests of both a global industry bent on maintaining its hegemony and aspirant states keen to join and benefit from it.

Introduction

0.1 What is a Global Clinical Trial?

However strong and widespread they may have become, expressions such as 'global companies', 'global networks' and 'global partnerships' cannot grasp the whole nature of very complex processes. Actors such as multinational companies are not only incapable of producing separate worlds in which local factors could be abolished, they also become less and less willing to do so. The more internationalized an economic activity, the more strongly it tends to depend on local resources and skills. It is this contemporary entanglement between global trends and local processes that is focused on in this book, by means of a socio-geographical analysis of multicentre clinical trials.

By global or multicentre trials,[1] I am referring to clinical research activities sponsored by multinational pharmaceutical companies and aimed to assess the efficacy and safety of new therapeutic compounds. Such studies can involve a small group of countries and sites,[2] but in many cases, large numbers of countries and sites are selected.

It is somewhat risky to present figures on global trials because many clinical studies are simply not published until the company submits its data to regulatory agencies. In addition, some scientific complexities can hinder a clear-cut classification and differentiation of clinical studies (Petryna 2009). In spite of such limitations, some figures provide us with glimpses of strikingly expanding processes. According to Petryna, for instance:

---

1   I use the expressions 'multicentre trials', 'global trials' and 'international trials'' as synonyms, for the distinction does not seem necessary in the framework of this book. Furthermore, I am not drawing a distinction between 'clinical trial', 'clinical study' and 'clinical research'.
2   A site is every location (such as hospitals, medical practices or research institutions) where clinical trials are conducted.

> *GlaxoSmithKline ran 29 percent of its trials outside the United States and Western Europe in 2004; by 2007, that figure grew to 50 percent. Wyeth Pharmaceuticals conducted half of its trials outside the United States in 2004; that figure rose to 70 percent in 2006 (Petryna 2009, p. 13).*

It is also known that in 2008, 60–70 per cent of the R&D investments made by pharmaceutical and biotech companies were directed to the conduct of clinical trials (Voi Consulting 2009).

Nowadays, all the top pharmaceutical companies offshore at least half of their clinical studies. As a result, even though the United States continues to concentrate about 75 per cent of the world's clinical studies (Fisher 2009, p. 2), it is not to 'traditional' regions (the United States and Western Europe) that we have to turn the eyes to find thriving examples, but instead to countries like Poland, India, China, South Africa or Brazil.

Probably, the most telling figures are similar to that which comes from the United States' Office of the Inspector General: 'the number of subjects involved in international clinical trials grew enormously from 4,000 in 1995 to 400,000 in 1999, according to partial estimates' (cited by Petryna 2009, p. 38). One of the reasons for this striking growth is the appearance of a new type of company specialized in the conduct of trials.

0.2 What is a CRO?

According to some analysts (Piachaud 2002; Mirowski and Van Horn 2005; Shuchman 2007; Fisher 2009), the globalization of clinical trials was extremely facilitated by the emergence of Clinical Research Organizations (CROs). These are companies that focus exclusively on clinical trials, offering a vast range of research services to pharma companies, from patient recruitment[3] to the analysis of a study's results.

Monitoring of sites, data management and statistics are the services that pharma companies most frequently hire from CROs. According to one of my interviewees, the Director for Patient Recruitment of a global CRO: 'That is the backbone of any CRO's services.' These services may involve the very

---

3   Recruitment is the set of activities through which patients are identified for, and enrolled in, clinical trials.

earliest phases of a trial's life, such as design of the clinical protocol.[4] Actually, there are three common situations. First, the CRO may receive a ready-made protocol from the sponsor[5] and becomes responsible for putting it into practice. Second, the pharma company may propose a draft protocol to be reviewed and improved by the CRO. Finally, the CRO may be given the responsibility for designing the whole protocol.

Efficiency and precision are the tenets of CROs, which pursue targets in such an adamant way that in certain research sites, they may end up being considered as too sturdy, market-driven actors (Fisher 2009). This rigid stance is sustained by the internal organization of CROs, which are composed of departments specializing in different aspects of trials (regulation, science, research infrastructure, among others). According to a physician-investigator whom I interviewed in Paris, the medical staff of a hospital would not be able to manage a clinical trial as efficiently as a CRO does:

> a CRO probably has higher and more experienced quality standards and the work it provides to the industry will probably be more in line with the industry's expectations. We are medical staff, some of us have recently finished the course; we may be like beginners in terms of our quality of service. A CRO is experienced; it does only that.

In addition to such technical expertise, CROs help to comply with certain regulations. In the European Union, for instance, a trial's sponsor must have local representation. As Lantrès (2007, p. 48) explains, 'the communitarian text creates the notion of "sponsor's legal representative", imposing to the sponsor that is not located in the European Union the designation of a representative in the region.' Thus, by hiring a CRO, pharma companies not based in Europe can access both a partner to conduct the study and a legal representative.

Classically, CROs are used to conduct very big trials. In other words: 'people come to us because they want the study done in lots of different countries', as a Vice-President for Clinical Management put it in an interview conducted in London. As the number of these big trials expands, CROs become increasingly needed. 'In 2004, the pharmaceutical industry reported outsourcing 57.5 percent of their studies to CROs' (Fisher 2009, p. 116). Actually, partnerships with CROs depend on the characteristics of the research site and the kind of

---

4   The protocol is the document guiding the conduct of a clinical trial.
5   The sponsor is the pharmaceutical company responsible for funding a clinical trial.

study undertaken there. In a private clinical research centre I visited in São Paulo, for example, about 50 per cent of studies are managed by CROs.

Even though some sites tend, or are more willing, to work directly with pharma companies, the relevance of CROs is an undeniable fact. The partnership between pharma companies and CROs forms a complex that I will refer to as the 'trials industry' following Fisher's (2009) usage. As this industry's eagerness to test and launch new drugs increase, research subjects[6] become highly treasured by these companies that are promoting a global 'hunting for experimental bodies' (Shah 2006, p. 39). However, as we shall see, from a sociological standpoint the access to bodies is not the most important issue to be taken into account. As soon as one focuses on social relations, flows of *communication* and the weight of local contexts, it is then possible to realize that the universe of multicentre trials is laden with questions which transcend the clinical and technical need for biological bodies.

0.3 Multicentre Trials and Social Actions

Since the mid-1990s, several analysts have studied the reasons why pharmaceutical companies have decided to globalize clinical studies. Such explanations can be separated into two groups. First, some authors put forward global factors leading companies to offshore their studies: the existence of lax regulatory frameworks in countries that are new to clinical research (Angell 1997, 2005; Shah 2006); the lower costs incurred by companies in those countries (Shah 2006; Dainesi and Elkis 2007; Fisher 2009); the statistical weight of trials involving large and ethnically diverse populations (Marschner 2010); the clinical weight of trials involving people who have precarious access to medicines, if at all, and whose bodies, therefore, hold few drug interactions, displaying the effects of candidate medicines more clearly (Petryna 2005). Second, there is a sociological approach that focuses on local factors, namely the pressures made by local actors (patients, activist groups, national regulatory institutions, among others) asking for more diverse studies in which ethnic minorities and people from several countries are recruited (Epstein 2007).

Each of these groups of explanations points to important factors in the globalization of trials, but they foreground either global or local phenomena. The point to be made in this book is that global trials are driven, at the same time, by global and local processes. Moreover, they are mainly fostered by

---

6   Research subjects are the (healthy or sick) people recruited for a clinical trial.

a paradox: they represent the encounter between two types of *rationalities* expressed by two groups of social actors speaking completely different languages and holding completely different expectations and views.

Thus, although this book draws on some contributions provided by previous studies, it is aimed to fill a gap that has been produced by these same studies, in which the interplay between global and local aspects has not been fully explored. The basic assumption of the proposed approach is the mundane fact that for a global trial to be undertaken, there must be multinational companies sponsoring and monitoring the study, on the one hand, and a research staff conducting it in particular sites, on the other. Each of these actors (multinational companies and research staff) brings particular rationales to the world of clinical research. To be more precise, it is possible to identify two types of *social action*.

On the one hand, multinational companies must perform strict calculations. The correct countries must be selected according to their overall research features (Petryna 2009), the most suitable statistical tools must be marshalled (Marschner 2010), and a whole set of clinical standards must be complied with (Timmermans and Berg 2003; Lakoff 2005). Eventually, a global trial constitutes a sort of *instrument* whose functioning has to be efficient both in terms of scientific evidence and economic performance. Thus I claim that *instrumental actions* can be identified.

> We term instrumental an action oriented towards success whenever we consider it from the point of view of the pursuit of technical rules of action and we assess the degree of efficiency of a given intervention in a context of states of things and events (Habermas 1987, p. 295).

On the other hand, the research staff's activities point to different issues. The conduct of a trial may represent, for physician-investigators and their institutions, the opportunity to gain scientific prestige or have access to substantial payments. At the same time, it may signify the access to cutting-edge therapies to fulfil medical responsibilities toward patients. Eventually, a global trial would be a sort of resource to solve immediate problems, and to provide the assistance that is needed by other social actors (patients). It is then possible to talk about *communicative actions* in trials.

> I speak of communicative actions whenever the plans of action of the participant actors are not coordinated by egocentric calculations of

success but by acts of intercomprehension. In the communication
activity, participants are not primordially oriented towards their own
success; they seek their individual goals with the condition that they
can reach mutual associations of their actions plans based on common
definitions of situations (Habermas 1987, p. 295).

Therefore, the theory of communicative action (Habermas 1987, 1996) can help scrutinize multicentre trials. However, I will make two original propositions. First, it is necessary to consider not only the presence of these two rationalities, but also the ways in which they mingle and overlap. Second, global and local actors can meet because of a whole chain of social *mediations* which enable them to cluster around clinical research activities. Hence the emergence of what I call *mediational action*. At the global and local pole of multicentre trials, one finds two different sets of languages, needs and expectations; in a word, two different *rationalities*. Therefore, the *mediational action* comes into play in order to enable a distant, albeit effective, dialogue between the discordant poles.[7]

By analysing the emergence and features of *mediational actions*, it is possible to consider both global and local aspects of clinical trials in a balanced way. In their struggle for social legitimacy and economic success, global actors seem to be less likely to succeed without relying on the support of these *mediational actions*, which allow them to anchor their actions into revitalizing local contexts.

0.4 Aims

The new relations between global and local actors, enabled by the emergence of the *mediational action*, is the focus of this book. The study of this phenomenon is important in understanding the society's features under the new conditions of capitalism. Nowadays, technologies marshalled within the global economy display an unprecedented capacity to shape and affect ordinary people's lives in local contexts. Even those activities that are deeply related to international prices and negotiations, such as oil prospecting, have already affected peoples' lives in disastrous ways, and some authors have even spoken of the emergence of a 'risk society' (Beck 2005; Nowotny, Scott and Gibbons 2007).

---

7   According to the Cambridge dictionary (www.dictionary.cambridge.org), mediation takes place when somebody talks 'to two separate people or groups involved in a disagreement to try to help them to agree or find a solution to their problems'. The term mediation is used in the domain of law, pointing to a form of alternative dispute resolution.

Adriana Petryna (2002), in her study on the atomic disaster in Chernobyl, was perhaps the first to realize that technical and scientific matters have acquired a new pervasive force, affecting the lives of many people, suddenly transformed into research subjects. Nowadays, the globalization of clinical research tends to normalize the principle of 'experimentality', which turns into a common aspect of everyday life (Marks 1997). The trend is reinforced by the fact that we are now dealing with an actual industry (a trials industry) endowed with international guidelines and adjusted to the economic and cultural traditions of several countries.

Thus it is now possible to mingle technical, scientific, and global matters with cultural, local concerns in a profound way. Moreover, these mixtures are facilitated by the emergence, at the local level, of actors and institutional arrangements that make local resources available to global actors. It is this new set of actions, mediating between the global and local scales, that is highlighted in this book. Globalization has been addressed in many studies, but some questions arise: what happens when a global enterprise (such as multicentre trials) starts drawing on the dynamics of medical institutions (such as hospitals) where people look for the solution of basic and vital needs? What are the impacts of global activities on these medical institutions? Are global actions undertaken in a separate space, in a world of their own, or do they have connections to local contexts?

The large numbers of studies on multicentre trials that have appeared over the last decades have allowed us to consider a growing range of aspects and consequences of clinical research. This book intends to reveal further aspects by means of two original methods. On the one hand, I am looking at trials by using the basic tenets of the theory of communicative action. On the other hand, instead of dealing with trials in all of their stages, we will focus on their initial stages (the 'start-up' process, in the CROs' jargon), in which studies are not yet running, investigators not yet dealing with clinical matters and research subjects not yet undergoing the study's procedures. It is in this stage that actors (institutions, caregivers, investigators, research subjects, among others) are selected; agreements are made and contracts signed; the geographical distribution of the study decided upon; and strategies of patient recruitment looked for. By focusing on this precise, early moment, it is possible to surprise the trials industry forging the social chains with which a clinical trial is made not only *scientifically* and *legally* feasible but also *socially* and *culturally* possible.

0.5 Methods, Fieldwork, and Limitations

The reflections presented here derive from two research projects. First, it is one of the outcomes of a Ph.D. study conducted at the Department of Political Economy, King's College London.[8] Second, I developed a study within the Drugs Exchange Program, a European Science Foundation networking initiative. With a travel grant, I developed fieldwork in Madrid (Spain) and Paris (France). Subsequently, I completed this study with a fieldwork in the UK, Brazil and South Africa. These countries were selected because of their relevance in the domain of global trials. The UK, Spain and France are 'traditional' locations for clinical research, being almost mandatory settings for the trials industry. Brazil and South Africa are countries displaying a steady rise in the reception of global studies. They are scientific and economic hubs in their regions, and have become pivotal settings for CROs, which tend to concentrate regional managing responsibilities there. Thus, in addition to involving five key situations, my study also focuses on three different world regions (Western Europe, South America and Southern Africa).

Along with the collection of information and data in libraries and other institutions, I interviewed several professionals involved with clinical research. For the identification of my interviewees, I consulted the American website clinicaltrials.gov (in which many key researchers and companies register most of the trials they are conducting), as well as the websites of hospitals. I collected the email addresses of research centres, principal investigators and co-investigators whenever this information was available. Then, I contacted those people by email or telephone.

In addition, two global CROs agreed to participate in my fieldwork. They are pivotal companies in the field of global trials, figuring on the list of the top ten global CROs. In all the five countries involved in my study, I visited the offices of these two companies and interviewed some of their employees. As they operate with standardized procedures, in all the countries I was dealing with the same organization of work or, to evoke an expression I used elsewhere (Bicudo 2006), the same 'organizational system.' Thus it was possible to see how those systems are adjusted according to national and local particularities.

---

8   The project 'Globalization and ideology: ethics committees and global clinical trials in South Africa and Brazil' was developed with a scholarship from Capes, a Brazilian funding agency, and supervised by Dr Alex Faulkner and Professor Brian Salter.

One of the CROs involved in my fieldwork has its headquarters in the United States and operates under very strict conditions in terms of standards and hierarchy. Indeed, by conducting my interviews, I realized that in many circumstances its employees ignored some procedures and information that, according to my expectation, would be part of their basic knowledge. In addition, these interviewees were very cautious in addressing some issues pertaining to the company's organization and strategies. In Madrid, for example, a Director for Site Management adopted, at a certain point in the interview, a clearly suspicious attitude, probably supposing that I, instead of being a Ph.D. student, would be an emissary of a competing company trying to discover business plans.

In the other CRO involved in my study (which has its global headquarters in Western Europe), things were fairly different. Although the interviewees did assume a cautious vein when dealing with some issues, they were more generous at disclosing information, in addition to being more knowledgeable of the company's procedures and operations. In other words, they might be depicted as less 'standardized employees' conveying less 'standardized discourses'. Even the monitors[9] I interviewed (one in Madrid and another one in São Paulo) demonstrated a very comprehensive notion about the company and the field of clinical trials. Some local managers even criticized certain aspects of this CRO's global organization. I did not have time to verify whether such differences between the two CROs have any impact on their relationship to sites, but my impression is that the second company may be more flexible in terms of standards, deadlines and procedures.

For the interviews, I used a structure which was slowly changed and improved in the course of the fieldwork. My questions were open and selected from my basic structure according to the function and time availability of the interviewee. Only two interviews were done by telephone. All the interviews were recorded (with permission from the interviewees) and conducted by the author in the local languages.[10] The longest interview lasted 82 minutes (in a CRO in Paris) and the shortest one, only 17 minutes (in a CRO in São Paulo). The average length was 40 minutes. Table I.1 summarizes the fieldwork of my study.

---

9   Monitors are professionals who visit research sites in order to make sure that everything is done according to the study's protocol. They occupy a low position in a CRO's hierarchy.

10 In the UK, the interviews were conducted in English; in Spain, Spanish; in France, French; in Brazil, Portuguese; and in South Africa, English, which is one of the eleven official languages of the country.

Table I.1   Summary of the fieldwork: interviewees

Country*	Period of the fieldwork	Staff of CROs	Principal investigators	Research coordinators	Co-investigators	Managers of private research centres	Others†	Total
UK	November 2010 to February 2011	5	1	1	1	0	4	12
Spain	October 2010	7	3	1	1	0	0	12
France	November 2010	7	6	0	0	0	0	13
Brazil	March to May 2011	8	5	7	0	1	1	22
South Africa	June to August 2011	6	2	1	0	2	6	17
Total	**November 2010 to August 2011**	**33**	**17**	**10**	**2**	**3**	**11**	**76**

* The fieldwork involved the following cities: in Spain, Madrid; in France, Paris; in the UK, London and other two cities (which I am not specifying to protect the companies' anonymity); in Brazil, São Paulo and Porto Alegre; in South Africa, Cape Town, Johannesburg and Pretoria.

† I am including here, for the UK: three people working in a private recruitment centre and one person working for the research unit of a hospital; for Brazil: the coordinator of a technological agency of a private university; and for South Africa: the director of a local CRO, a research pharmacist, a nurse, and the recruitment manager and two regulatory managers of a non-governmental organization (NGO).

Table I.2   Summary of the fieldwork: research sites and institutions

Country	Offices of two global CROs	State hospital or clinic	Private hospital or practice	Private clinical trial centre*	Others†	Total
UK	2	5	0	1	0	8
Spain	2	2	1	1	0	6
France	2	6	0	0	0	8
Brazil	2	5	3	1	1	12
South Africa	3‡	2	0	2	5	12
Total	**11**	**20**	**4**	**5**	**6**	**48**

* Here I am including: for the UK: a recruitment centre; and for South Africa: a global Site Management Organisation (SMO), and a private company located within a state hospital.

† I am including here: for Brazil: a technological agency of a private university; for South Africa: a clinical research centre of a state university, a local CRO, two local NGOs, and the department of pharmacology of a state university.

‡ In all the countries, I visited the same two global CROs. In South Africa, however, I visited the offices of one of these companies in two different cities.

For the interview analysis, I listened to the recordings, transcribing (and when needed, translating into English) the most relevant parts. Thus each interview was converted into a five- or six-page-long Word document. Quotes and data were organized according to relevant themes, then these documents were consulted during the writing process. I will not differentiate between the two CROs studied. In my text, I have almost transformed them into a single company, which is focused on in order to exemplify the logics and operations of CROs in general.

I am deeply grateful to all those people who kindly and wholeheartedly agreed to sacrifice some slots of their busy timelines for the benefit of my study. I am totally convinced that the politically troublesome (and sometimes disastrous) nature of global clinical trials is the outcome of a system of social actions, having nothing to do with the intentions of these serious professionals. My study was reviewed by an ethics committee[11] and, therefore, I am not disclosing either the interviewees' names or the name of their institutions or companies. In some instances, this is a regrettable procedure because disclosing the name of some hospitals would help unravel phenomena and make information more meaningful.

The compliance with this confidentiality rule is, therefore, the first limitation of my study. Second, it is limited by its qualitative nature, for although I conducted interviews and observations in pivotal companies and institutions, I am focusing on a relatively small number of empirical examples. Finally, I am somewhat limited by moral commitments towards my interviewees. Indeed, in some cases the contribution I had from those people went beyond the provision of some information through long and detailed interviews. In South Africa, for instance, due to the precarious condition of public transport, I accepted to be taken, by the driver of a company, from Johannesburg to an office in Pretoria. This type of help was rare in my fieldwork but in several situations, my interviewees were more than trustful towards me and disclosed more than they might probably have done. Thus in spite of my critical view about the organization of multicentre trials, I should comply with a moral obligation and be cautious at certain moments, unravelling and stressing what is politically and sociologically relevant but without revealing strategies and choices that belong to the companies' business secrets.

---

11 King's College London ethics committee.

0.6 The Structure of the Book

My text is structured in two main parts. In the first, the institutional dimension of multicentre trials is highlighted, through an analysis of the relations between research sites and investigators on the one hand, and the trials industry, on the other. The first chapter focuses on the global standards of the industry and their impact on the work organization of sites. It is shown that, from the viewpoint of medical institutions, the arrival of global studies implies not only the assimilation of some technical procedures but a deep upheaval in their material, social and ideological configurations. In order to further explore this issue, Chapter 2 highlights the financial dimension of trials, which has been poorly explored in previous studies. We shall see that in spite of the formulation of some institutional tools aimed to control payments and reimbursements, there is still much leeway for unclear arrangements in the field of multicentre trials. In Chapter 3, the physicians' standpoint is stressed, in order to show that clinical studies provide these professionals with some opportunities to fulfil their medical tasks.

The second part explores the geographical face of global trials, drawing attention to three different scales. In Chapter 4, we stress the urban dynamics of trials, showing how these studies draw on a series of infrastructures, creations and *flows of communication* that can only be found in big cities. In the fifth chapter we focus on the national scale, analysing the competitions and hierarchies created by the trials industry. Finally, the sixth chapter deals with cultural aspects of trials (which also belong to the geographical space). We shall see that the economic and technical vitality of trials also depends on sets of expectations and fragilities faced by both physicians and patients. In the conclusion, we revisit some reflections undertaken throughout the book.

0.7 What is Schrödinger's Cat?

To a great extent, the analysis of multicentre trials, from a socio-geographical and communicative point of view, demands an ability to deal with paradoxes. In 1935, Austrian physicist Erwin Schrödinger proposed a theoretical model that was to become one of the most famous examples of paradox in the history of science. According to the explanation that had been proposed by quantum physics, atoms can display superposed states. By formulating mathematical functions, physicists had shown that it is not worth asking if an atom is stable *or* disintegrated (decayed) at any particular moment, for it is always, *at the same time*, stable *and* decayed. Bearing this explanation in mind, Schrödinger imagined a cat inside a box with a killing mechanism whose functioning depended on the structure of an atom. If the atom decayed, the mechanism would be activated, killing the cat. As the mathematical function of quantum physics tells us that the atom is, at the same, stable *and* decayed, then the cat inside the box can only be, at the same time, dead *and* alive.

This provocative and sharp model pointed out an important dilemma. On the one hand, the cat's life must be explained and described by classical physical approaches. On the other, the atom's structure asks for novel explicative approaches, deriving from quantum physics. As in Schrödinger's times (and things have not changed since then) there was no way to reconcile or unify these two interpretations, the only solution was to consider that, in a sense, the cat is indeed dead *and* alive.

In social sciences, straight and rigid ways of thinking are sometimes mobilized. Looking for seemingly coherent explanations, some analysts tend to avoid paradoxes, even though the contemporary world tends to be laden with them. Eventually, the need for coherence may lead to one-sided, biased explanations. In this book, I try to construct an interpretation that instead of escaping the paradox, accepts it and takes it as the raw material of sociological inquiry. By focusing on multicentre clinical trials, I strive to grasp the coexistence of rationalities, a phenomenon that, according to my interpretation, is the main feature of our times.

At the global level, it is important to comprehend the operations of multinational companies, those cats whose footprints are modifying the features of many national territories and societies. At the local level, it is necessary to consider the relevance of local actors and social relations whose minimal and atomic dynamics challenge our classical thought. When these two sets of actors meet, unexpected phenomena and unforeseen events do emerge. Thus, by crossing the two parts composing this book, the reader may have the impression that we are oscillating between two approaches to the same story, and each time proposing divergent conclusions. If this impression really comes into play, there is no need to fabricate any reconciling coherence and claim that the cat is dead *or* alive. The entanglements between global and local actions have become so strong that, as it seems to me, there is nothing to do but consider that the cat is, at the same time, dead *and* alive.

In this book, the cat will sometimes be deadly alive, nourished by the global standards of *instrumental actors*. The same cat will subsequently be lively dead, when the surprising features of *communicative actors* is unveiled. The paradox is insurmountable, for everything depends on the choices made by *mediational actors* who can be either *implicitly* involved in *conspiracies* with the trials industry or *explicitly* driven by the *democratic* features of their local contexts.

PART ONE

Global Trials in Medical Institutions

Infrastructure: The Indirect Privatization of Hospitals

In multicentre trials, the international reach of CROs and pharma companies requires the establishment of several types of standards, so that activities and outcomes can be normalized and compared. Hospitals are turned into sites; patients into research subjects; individual sufferings into cases. We are dealing with the sociological phenomenon of 'commensuration', as defined by Espeland and Stevens (1998, p. 316): 'Commensuration transforms qualities into quantities, difference into magnitude. It is a way to reduce and simplify disparate information into numbers that can easily be compared.'

As Lakoff (2005) pointed out, standardization and commensuration are typical to medical thought, which frames diseases as stable phenomena existing outside the body. In clinical trials, this abstract approach is reinforced because there must be a vast range of standards ruling procedures and ways of measuring events. Clinical protocols 'standardize a set of practices, actors, and situations. They intervene in a specified situation and prescribe a set of activities that should be performed in a similar way in order to achieve results comparable over time and space' (Timmermans and Berg 2003, p. 63).

The first and most general manifestation of standardization in trials is the emergence of international rules that submit several countries to the same clinical and regulatory procedures. In 1964, the Declaration of Helsinki mandated broad ethical parameters (Fisher 2009), and was subsequently reshaped by the interests of multinational companies (Shah 2006).

Petryna (2009) provides us with many other examples of how regulatory standardization advanced in clinical trials: in the early 1990s, pharmaceutical companies formulated a new set of guidelines through the creation of the International Conference on Harmonization, launched in tandem with the Trips

Agreement;[1] many systems and institutions have mushroomed all over the world, as is the case of ethics committees; the Food and Drug Administration (the United States regulatory agency) has audited sites in many countries, thereby enforcing the global diffusion of some standards; in 1995, the world witnessed the creation of GCP: 'The GCP (Good Clinical Practice) is a set of World Health Organization guidelines for the design, conduct, performance, monitoring, auditing, recording, analysis, and reporting of clinical trials' (Petryna 2009, pp. 107–108).

As a result of this process, the field of clinical trials has turned into an internationalized regulatory environment (Rozovsky and Adams 2003; Abraham 2007, 2009). The trend is reinforced because in many countries 'the pharmaceutical industry was, and is, permitted to have privileged strategic access to, and involvement with, government regulatory policy over and above any other interest group' (Abraham 2009, p. 58).

The goal of this chapter is not to analyse the occurrence of standardization in clinical trials, as this has already been successfully carried out (Gray 1975; Timmermans and Berg 2003). Here, I try to unravel the impacts of standardization and commensuration upon particular hospitals involved in global trials. We shall see that standards can have both positive and disturbing outcomes, depending on how, and by whom, they are installed. Moreover, we shall see that the proliferation of standards ends up creating series of regulatory loopholes, which open up some leeway for hidden negotiations in multicentre trials. Slowly, research activities conducted in medical institutions become less and less subject to decisions taken in state agencies, and the trials industry seems to take over these responsibilities, fostering a process of indirect privatization of hospitals.

We begin this analysis with a brief overview of recent regulatory renewals experienced by the five countries included in my study. We move on to focusing on the global standards that CROs implement and comply with. Subsequently, the so-called feasibility studies are analysed. Then, we begin to focus on the impacts of global standards on the organization of hospitals, starting this analysis with the rhythms of work imposed by the industry. We continue by addressing the quantitative concerns promoted in multicentre trials. After discussing the ways in which hospitals equip themselves for the arrival of international trials, we focus on the hospitals' human resources. Then, the

---

1   The 'Trade Related Aspects of Intellectual Property (TRIPS)' agreement accompanied the creation of the World Trade Organization in 1994.

partnerships between hospitals and the trials industry are studied. Finally, I stress the deep association between private companies and state hospitals, as well as the emergence of a new *reality* in medical institutions.

1.1 National Regulatory Renewals

In all of the five countries we are studying here (the UK, Spain, France, Brazil and South Africa), it is possible to identify approximately the same regulatory structures: national laws of clinical research, regulatory agencies, and ethics committees, among others. To be sure, there are differences pertaining to the pace of the regulatory process and the internal organization of institutions, but the fundamentals of these national systems do not vary substantially.

In South Africa, ethics committees[2] have appeared sparingly, because many hospitals delegate the review of their studies to other sites (Bicudo 2012). It is the only country in our 'sample' where private ethics committees are of important weight.[3] In 1996 South Africa published the National Policy on Medicines, whose guidelines were addressed in detail by the 2003 Act 59, in which national legislation was brought into line with international rules. Today the Medicines Control Council is the regulatory agency responsible for authorizing clinical trials, whereas the National Health Research Ethics Council is the principal ethics body, responsible for registering and certifying ethics committees.

The Brazilian regulatory framework was also changed in 1996, when the National Commission for Research Ethics (*Comissão Nacional de Ética em Pesquisa*) was created as one of the measures mandated by Resolution 196, which addressed ethical and practical procedures of clinical research. The Resolution fostered the proliferation of ethics committees in several hospitals and, as a result, Brazil has today more than 600 ethics committees. The National Agency for Sanitary Surveillance (*Agência Nacional de Vigilância Sanitária*) is the main regulatory body.

---

2   Ethics committees are collective bodies responsible for analysing (from an ethical point of view) research proposals submitted by the trials industry and individual investigators. Generally, they are responsible for studies conducted at a particular site.

3   By 'private ethics committees', I mean committees that are not affiliated to a hospital or university, being established as small companies specializing in the ethical review of research protocols.

The situations of the UK, Spain and France can be studied together, for these countries have participated in a regional effort of regulatory harmonization. In 2001, the European Parliament approved the Directive 2001/20, which created regional rules for the conduct of clinical trials. As Marchal (2007) explains, the Directive aims to both encourage the implementation of good clinical practices and harmonize the procedures mandated by the different countries. As a consequence, national procedures to process research applications are slowly becoming similar, enabling, for instance, the approximation of the timelines followed by ethics committees and regulatory agencies.

In 2004, the Directive was transposed to the British, Spanish and French laws. In the UK, the shift was realized by the Medicines for Human Use Regulations; in Spain, the transposition happened through a Royal Decree; France adopted the Directive's rules by means of a Law of Public Health that was complemented by a 2006 decree. While the UK and Spain have ethics committees attached to research sites, France holds a system of regional committees, whose number amounts to only 40.

Thus the trials industry is aware that in spite of some differences, these five countries are operating under the same basic conditions. The modernization of national regulatory frameworks creates a sort of international language that is more than suitable for companies such as global CROs. In the next section, we analyse how they have been implementing global standards of work and therefore producing a type of abstract space of their own.

1.2 The Global Space of Multinational CROs

In 2011 the Brazilian government began to renew its regulations pertaining to clinical trials. The initiative would imply, in a first moment, shifts in the so-called Regulation 196, which guides the conduct of clinical studies. In the UK, I interviewed a CRO's Global Manager who was aware of the changes in Brazil. According to him, 'we're lobbying and we're working with the Brazilian Ministry of Health to be able to make it more competitive in being involved in clinical trials'. This interest is understandable, for the more similar national legislations the more appropriate the operational field of multinational actors becomes. As a result of such globalizing trends, a regulatory framework tends to be globally constructed and as Espeland and Stevens (1998) claimed, it becomes difficult to sustain the force of local rules.

If shaping national rules is a tricky aim for multinational companies to achieve, the formulation of global procedures to be followed within a company is much simpler. In an interview in Madrid, a CRO's Director of Clinical Operations summarized the tenets of global companies:

> We work with global procedures. Theoretically, the vast majority of our work procedures are global ones and valid all over the world. Then there is a set of procedures that are specific to regions (Europe, America, Asia or Africa) and then there are a few procedures that are specific to the country ... Because, of course, there are some procedures that depend on local regulations. But I would say that 90 per cent or more of our work is of global procedures; they are the same all over the world.

The implementation of global standards of work has to do with the economic efficiency sought by multinational companies, which would incur high costs if they were to realize drastic adjustments in different countries. As a CRO's Vice-President for Global Patient Recruitment claimed: 'it doesn't make a lot of sense to be doing ... one system in Asia and another system in North America and a different system in Europe'. The search for rationality and efficiency may lead to extreme examples of standardization, such as the layout of CROs' offices, which must have the same appearance and functionality regardless of the country.

However, such details are nothing but expressions of more fundamental issues relating to the CROs' organization of work, such as the formation of departments and teams. As long as the most decisive and strategic operations (such as the financial management of studies) remain centralized in global headquarters, the constitution of globally widespread teams can be economically interesting. Indeed, CROs' employees are often selected from different countries, or even continents, to form a team dealing with specific matters. As a British Vice-President for Clinical Management explained to me: 'most of the communication on running a study is international rather than national'. Technologies such as email or teleconferences are of paramount importance for people who can be in more frequent touch with their counterparts in distant countries than with other people working on a different floor of the same building. In Johannesburg, for example, I interviewed a Contract Specialist who spends about 50 per cent of her work time dealing with contracts to be signed in Europe. Such phenomena enhance the international flow of personnel between different units of a company. According to a Director of Clinical Management interviewed in São Paulo:

I've already had monitors transferred to the office in Canada, the office in the United States, some managers were also transferred, and they leave here and the following day they are working there ... And it is like exactly the same procedures, exactly the same training, the adaptation is immediate.

For these nomadic workers, language is not an issue. I interviewed a British Director of Clinical Management who spent some years in China; and a South African CEO who lived in Brazil for three years. Both persons did not become able to communicate in the local languages, for they used English in their everyday tasks. Indeed, the field of multicentre trials witnessed the emergence of a global vocabulary not only because of the globalization of procedures, standards and schemes; because the flow of data and information between various countries must be rapid and precise, a global language is in need, and English has been elected to play this role.

As Santos (1979) pointed out, multinational companies tend to have few relationships in the places they are based in. By analysing the case of CROs, one might even have the impression of floating companies for which the surrounding situation would be of minimal relevance. For those who are engaged in the everyday tasks of CROs, an eventual feeling of geographical indifference may be experienced. This is, for instance, the declaration of a Director of Clinical Operations interviewed in Madrid:

The geographical location is almost meaningless. As our studies are international, a monitor who is based in Spain has a clinical study manager who may be in Belgium, the project manager may be in the United States and the person who is responsible for regulatory issues may be in Sweden and the physician who is responsible for the trial may be in another country.

As we shall see,[4] such impressions of geographical indifference are not underpinned by careful analyses that can reveal the strong dependency the trials industry has toward local actors and creations.

Obviously, the proliferation of international standards has its implications. On the one hand, the global organization of CROs leads to economic and technical efficiency. On the other, it provokes misconceptions and a dearth of knowledge. For instance, professionals who are responsible for overseeing

---

4   In Chapter 4.

global operations are sometimes likely to ignore national particularities that are crucial to the conduct of a study. One example was given by a CRO's Contract Specialist interviewed in São Paulo. She told me that in some cases, the global legal department cannot help her team to deal with specific legal issues:

> *Apart from the support you get from the legal department, do you sometimes have to look for any external support?*[5]

> *Yes, because the legal department of our company, which serves Latin America, is based in the United States. So they basically know the legislation of the United States. So when we need some support relating to the local legislation, either of Brazil or other countries (because we are also responsible for other Latin American countries), then we contact some local lawyers, which are law offices that offer services to us.*

Thus CROs have created, through their operations, a sort of abstract global space that, being continuously reiterated and revisited, is sometimes more real than the concrete locations of their offices. On the one hand, we are dealing with companies whose global organization prevents a full commitment to the dynamics of the places in which they are installed. On the other hand, these very same companies are many times dictating procedures to be complied with by local actors. In Johannesburg, for instance, I visited a local CRO, a small company in the first years of its existence. According to its managing director, the company must strive to apply standards and procedures similar to those of multinational CROs. This is so 'because pretty much the [pharma] companies expect the same standard and there is no excuse if you're a small company or a large company'. Imitating the procedures of multinational CROs becomes a requisite for small CROs' survival. For research sites and whole countries, the weight of global standards can be even stronger, as we shall see in the following sections.

1.3 What are Feasibility Studies?

In global pharmaceutical research there are initial questions to ask: where are trials meant to be conducted? In what regions, countries and cities? Under the auspices of what institutions and professionals? In order to address these questions, CROs have developed an ingenious system called 'feasibility study'.

---

5   In some quotes from interviews I include my questions to make the information more meaningful. My speech is quoted in bold italics.

The process, which often takes one month to be concluded, can be either sold by CROs as a separate service or included into the package of services that pharma companies buy. Three procedures belong to this process.

> First, as a Feasibility Manager working in Paris explained to me: 'The goal of feasibility [studies] is first of all to know what the best countries are to participate in a study.' To be selected for a trial, a country must meet many requisites: an important occurrence of the targeted disease; appropriate expertise of medical institutions; that particular kind of study being in line with local regulations; the moral acceptance of that type of trial by physicians and lay people; among others.[6] The same interviewee gave me two examples of how a trial could be at odds with the medical traditions of a country:For instance, there is a study on a new treatment for hypertension but patients must have already been treated with medicine x. If medicine x is never used in France or very seldom used in France, I will say: 'Look, this study is not made for France.' Besides, if, for instance, there is a study on cancer which asks for a biopsy every month to verify what happens, I will say: 'This is not possible. It's not possible in France. In France one does not do a biopsy every month. Patients will never accept doing a biopsy every month; or physicians will say that.'

Second, feasibility studies have to do with the selection of institutions to run the trial. Once again, the choice of hospitals involves many criteria, the available infrastructure and the recruitment potential being the first ones.[7]

The third help that companies have from feasibility studies has to do with the identification of physician-investigators able to recruit large numbers of research subjects. A crucial instrument of the process is the so-called feasibility form, which is sent to investigators so that they describe the structure they have to conduct the study, and how many people with the required health condition they see per month or per year. Bearing this information in mind, one gets the number of patients that might be put into the study.

Clearly, by means of feasibility forms, investigators can do nothing but estimate the number of participants to be enrolled. It is always hard, if not impossible, to foresee what will happen in the actual recruitment process. What is more, at the moment of the feasibility study, investigators are often given

---

6   Other factors will be addressed in Chapter 5.
7   We come back to this point in subsequent sections of this chapter.

little information about the study. Obviously, they are informed the criteria for including and excluding patients,[8] but even this information may change during the recruitment process.

Therefore, while filling in the feasibility form, investigators may overestimate their recruitment potential in order to force their participation in a trial from which good economic or scientific results are expected. In Madrid, a CRO's Director for Clinical Management said: 'often in Spain, the investigators ... tend to be quite optimistic and say that they will recruit more than they usually recruit'. In Johannesburg, a Clinical Manager told me that overestimations are normal in South African private sites, and the reason is clear-cut: 'For business. 'Cause they get paid for trials.' However, there can be other reasons. For instance, a Clinical Manager based in Paris attributed the French investigators' optimism to their dedicating little time to the feasibility study and therefore not anticipating limiting factors of the recruitment process.

Thus a paradoxical situation emerges from feasibility studies. Although they are intended to help the trials industry make accurate decisions pertaining to the study's locations, they end up being a novel source of uncertainties, for it is impossible to produce the ideal outcome of the process: a precise selection of the most suitable sites.

The trials industry, whose main components (pharma companies and CROs) are *instrumental* actors par excellence, needs to manage uncertain situations by artificially producing some type of controllability. One scapegoat has been the formulation of statistical assessments which can be realized in some clinical sites. The following quote comes from an interview conducted in London with a psychologist, member of a research team dedicated to smoking-related diseases; we were talking about the number of patients that may be enrolled for a protocol:

And how can you estimate this number?

So, you use the calculations from previous studies. Yes. So, it would be kind of statistically worked out and. ... how many subjects you need in each condition to be able to get a significant outcome. But also you try to incorporate what would be the chance of, say, drop out depending on what field you're looking at. So we know, for example, from people that get recruited, you're probably looking at 30 per cent of those people

---

8   On the inclusion and exclusion criteria, see section 3.4.

might not turn out for the first clinic session ... But that is all done quite scientifically.

Thus some sites have used statistical tools in order to improve the estimations of the feasibility process. In some cases, the industry can even sponsor physicians to conduct small studies on the incidence of diseases within a hospital's area. With such data, it is easier to rapidly identify sites that might be good recruiters for particular trials. Nevertheless, these attempts are immediately limited by the unstable features of diseases and health care, as can be seen with an example given by a CRO's monitor in Madrid:

> **Can there be situations in which they [the investigators] say: 'Oh, we have 50 patients [for a clinical trial]' and this is not true?**
>
> *It may occur. For example, seasonal trials. The flu. 2009 was the year of type A flu ... Everybody went to the hospital. The number of cases increased. So if they thought: 'How many flu patients do I have?' A lot.*
>
> *... I went to a site to ask how many flu patients they would have for the following year and the estimation they did was based on the year of 2009. It is wrong. The flu is likely to be more virulent, more serious, or less ... Investigators don't lie, but reality is different.*

This example shows us that an endless complementarity is installed. Uncertainties lead to the use of calculations and statistical tools, which instead of enabling certainties produce new types of fluctuations and errors. As a result, even in those sites having good informational infrastructure, the assessments required by feasibility studies continue to be done 'more by experience than through precise calculations or simulations', as a French physician told me.

Feasibility studies define a sort of negotiation between the trials industry and investigators, because numbers must be anticipated, communicated and trusted. Economic interests may emerge here because depending on the number of participants recruited for a study, an investigator can have access to bigger payments or acquire the right to figure in the list of authors of a scientific publication.[9] Thus a sort of bargain may take place, in which investigators try to maximize their scientific or monetary benefits whereas the industry strives to take advantage of its dealing with many sites at the same time.

---

9   On these issues, see section 1.5.

Using Habermas'(1996) concepts, it is possible to say that clinical trials are composed not only by rigid protocols and standards (*facticity*) but also by uncertain negotiations and contextual factors (*validity*). The basic phenomenon which opens up some leeway for negotiations to happen is a scheme that I name 'source agreement'. I am referring to the fact that global trials are established, in the first place, as a result of negotiations between a company and an individual investigator. In terms of monetary matters, source agreements involve, on the one hand, a physician willing to get payments that justify his or her research effort and, on the other, a pharma company searching for maximizing financial benefits and therefore expanding profits. The CRO is the actor responsible for intermediating such dialogues.

The outcomes of source agreements are as uncertain as the estimations done in feasibility forms. In addition, the process takes place away from any type of *institutional* scrutiny apart from that which is undertaken by the industry and the investigators themselves. Consequently, as we shall see in the following sections, the leeway for technical and political decisions is enlarged, bringing an ever-growing flexibility to the core of multicentre trials.

1.4 Criteria to Include or Exclude Sites

In order to enjoy a close rapprochement to pharma companies, CROs can use the velocity of their procedures as an argument to conquest more studies. According to a Director for Patient Recruitment interviewed in the UK, 'we are moving more to these partnership deals and to risk-based contracts where we'll say [to pharma companies]: "Give us the work. If we deliver it ahead of schedule, you pay us a bonus; if we don't, then we get penalties in the contract."'

Necessarily, velocity becomes an imperative not only to CROs but also to research sites, which become also responsible for allowing clinical results to be handled 'ahead of schedule'. According to Vallejo (2006, pp. 189–190), hospitals are considered as ideal sites whenever they possess 'the capacity to realize a quick recruitment of patients' and manage to 'obtain a high number of patients'.

Indeed, hospitals have to follow the rhythm of new clocks when they start working in multicentre trials, for the industry's rigid timelines must be applied by their research partners as well. The Clinical Research Manager of a

London hospital spoke of the difference between academic studies[10] and trials sponsored by the industry:

> *with pharmaceutical companies, quite often, they want everything here, they want everything now, they want to know why the recruitment is not the rate that you're expected to be at and, you know, sort of [snapping the fingers] quick, quick, quick.*

This is a very telling way to depict the 'contemporary acceleration' that according to Santos (2000a), characterizes today's capitalism.

Apart from acting rapidly, sites must be capable of delivering great numbers. Obviously, the sites' productivity is not a factor that CROs gauge in an intuitive, approximate way. Over the last decade, they have developed informational tools in order to assess their partners' recruitment performances as accurately as possible. The initial procedures of this process were described, in Madrid, by a Director of Site Management:

> *Is there a manner of assessing a site's recruitment potential quantitatively?*

> *Of course ... When you assess a hospital, what you also assess is the population that is served. 'Does this hospital serve a population of 30,000 inhabitants or 300,000 or almost one million?' ... And then you do a more detailed study, that is: 'Of this population, how many go to the hospital and how often?' So you do a study, an analysis by services, by departments ... And that gives you an idea about the recruitment potential you can have, in addition to some tools that our company has in order to verify the historical performance of a certain site over many years.*

These 'tools', mobilized to verify the sites' 'historical performance', were described in another interview conducted in Madrid, with a Director for Site Identification:

> *What is done to evaluate the recruitment capacity [of sites]?*

> *Well, generally, we look at our database. We have historical information about how these hospitals and investigators have operated in different*

---

10   Academic studies are conducted by independent investigators, generally with funding from public institutions and no direct commercial applicability.

studies they have participated in. In this way, if somebody asks me: 'Can you identify some sites for myocardial infarct in Europe?' I go to the database, look for myocardial infarct and get data about investigators who have participated in studies with us. Then, this same worksheet gives me information about how many [participants] they have recruited ... Then, it tells you, in comparison to other investigators that took part in the same study, what their recruitment has been ... And it does that by considering the time they have had to recruit, also in comparison to others, and the number [of patients] they have recruited. If there is a site that had only one week to put ten patients, its percentage will be much higher than one that had one year and recruited ten patients as well.

Indeed, one the main CROs' tools is their clinical database, in which information is stored about institutions and clinical investigators. A CRO's Manager showed me one such global database, which enables broad and narrow searches to be done by country, city, disease, and type of institution, among other criteria. For each investigator, there is information on the medical specialties in which the person can run trials, as well as contact details. Furthermore, there is precise information about the investigators' recruitment performances in previous trials. Thus it is possible to know whether the company is dealing with someone who has a big recruitment potential or not. In the UK, a Director for Site Management told me about investigators: 'If they don't recruit for us on a project, then the likelihood of us going to use them again in the future is reduced significantly.'

Therefore, in order to cope with the uncertainties of trials, CROs recur to informational tools that enhance the role played by *facticity* in the selection of sites. Thus as Santos (2000a) argued, information has become a sort of energy without which the global companies' operations are stifled.

Generally, during the recruitment process CROs send newsletters to sites, so that research teams compare their performance to that of other teams. Arguably, this may serve as a means to foster concerns with timelines and targets. Eventually, medical professionals are forced to abide by the rhythms of global companies. The loss of payments, publications and scientific prestige are the common penalties for those which come to be framed as slow recruiters. As we shall see, numbers and targets come to be normalized in the *mental life* of hospitals.

1.5 What is 'n'?

By joining multicentre trials, hospitals have to slowly assimilate the *instrumental rationality*, manifested by means of targets, deadlines and many sorts of standards. To be sure, there are cases in which the demands of the trials industry can be done in quite direct ways, as in the example given by a CRO monitor interviewed in São Paulo:

> There was a moment in which I said: 'Doctor, you cannot continue with only your team of physicians because your physician, today, is seeing patients, sending laboratory samples to the central laboratory, filling in forms to send me by the end of the week ... The guy cannot do everything, so you must organize yourself to have research coordinators, equipments you need to have, and physicians to take care of patients.' And so he did and he improved a lot; he even turned into the high enroller[11] of the study in Brazil.

If such demands, voiced from a monitor to a physician in such a direct way, can sound too invasive and maybe even harsh, it is important to point out that the trials industry generally imposes procedures and standards with much more subtlety. For instance, CROs are gradually teaching caregivers to adopt new ways of thinking and organizing things. According to a Spanish Director of Clinical Operations:

> What we do is that ... we ask them [physician-investigators] to draw a recruitment plan, which is signed in the very first visit. With this recruitment plan ... we oblige the physician to seat down and think: 'How many potential patients do I have? How many would fit the criteria? Which other departments of the hospital will be involved? Will they help me? Yes or no? Who can send me patients from outside of the hospital?'

Encouraging physicians and research teams to consider all aspects of a trial in a strategic way amounts to instilling a *rationality* that is alien to the basic features of medical care and local needs. In order to enforce this rationality, CROs mobilize a dire number of monitors who visit sites regularly to make sure that international standards are complied with. Fisher (2009, pp. 100–101) is therefore right to claim: 'Monitoring becomes a mechanism to enforce

---

11 The site that manages to put the biggest number of subjects into a trial in a particular country.

rationality and accountability.' Indeed, an *instrumental rationality* starts springing from global actors to the realm of local actors, a phenomenon that is clearly expressed by the issue of the size of study populations. A physician based in a hospital in London summarized the way in which he determines the size of the study population for his own academic studies:

> *I start with the prior analysis or the prior study. I do the prior study just to prove the concept. I would look at what the expected difference [between the study arms[12]] is. And then, from there, I design a relatively small trial, 15, 20, 30 patients, just to generate the pilot data and, based on the pilot data, I would go into the main trial. And the main trial requires the prior analysis. I would take the literature, look at differences, I would take other larger trials. And I do the prior analysis and the prior analysis will tell me how many patients I need [for the main trial].*

In global companies' offices, the design of trials is realized in a quite similar fashion. Thus the *n*, that is, the number of subjects to be recruited for a clinical trial, is decided upon. The next step is the conduct of feasibility studies[13] in order to decide which countries and sites can participate.

This quantitative dimension of trials is crucial to pharma companies and CROs, as they have statistical and economic targets to reach. Thus numeric concerns end up crossing out the whole structures of these companies. In Paris, for example, a Site Identification Manager acknowledged that for her career within the CRO, it is important that France keeps being a good recruiter in multicentre trials. In a sense, French sites recruit for their own benefit, but also for the sake of the CRO's employees overseeing recruitment activities in the country. The declaration of a British Director for Site Management is very meaningful:

> *my mantra to my team has always been: 'If what you're doing right now doesn't contribute to greater patient numbers in the clinical studies either now or in the fairly near future, stop what you're doing and do something that will.'*

---

12 Arms are the groups into which a study population is divided. Some arms will take the candidate medicine, others receive either the standard therapy or a placebo.
13 On feasibility studies, see section 1.3.

The issue of the *n*, which is initially a major concern for global companies, pervades the whole system of trials until the point at which different professionals, in different countries and medical institutions, are also concerned with this quantitative aspect. Surreptitiously, there emerges a sort of 'marginal value' and 'marginal cost of research subjects', because it is known that each additional participant demands further efforts but increases the monetary payments made within a study.

In multicentre trials, the *n* has monetary implications because payments made to investigators and their teams depend on the number of subjects enrolled for the study (Fisher 2009). The bigger the number of people recruited, the higher the payments to investigators will be. Thus the investigators' decisions may end up being decisively informed by such monetary aspects. A physician who is based in a key hospital in Madrid disclosed to me some of his colleagues' mindset. According to him, most physician-investigators would prefer to join studies in which the workload is small, whereas payments per patient recruited are high.

Another physician who works in London told me that he participates in trials whenever 'I want to make a little bit of money so that I have something in my research pot to send my fellows [people of his research team] to conferences.' In addition to studies in which he plays the role of P.I. (principal investigator), this physician provides cardiologic imaging services for other studies. In these cases, the number of participants in the trial is one of the most decisive factors he considers. From his point of view, it is not worth delivering services for a study with few participants because there is much effort to be made (analysing the protocol, going to meetings, undertaking examinations, among other tasks) and little economic compensation to receive. Indeed, many aspects, including the number of patients to recruit, may end up being considered as factors of a calculation. For example, this description comes from an interview with the director of a private clinical trials centre in São Paulo.

> *For example, in a study on osteoporosis, the patient would come to the [research] centre about three times a year for appointments. It is more or less once in four months. A patient with rheumatoid arthritis comes every month. So if you consider that one of them comes once every four months, or three times a year, and the other one comes once a month, or twelve times a year, then one patient with rheumatoid arthritis is equal to four patients with osteoporosis, in terms of demand for me, demand of team and infrastructure I need to have.*

Eventually, such rationale frames people in terms of costs and benefits. For some physicians, the *n* has even become the main criterion to be considered before joining trials. This issue was addressed by the Managing Director of a South African CRO:

> *For example, there is one site in Cape Town, if you're doing a dermatology study ... She [the physician] won't participate in the feasibility study unless you tell her she can have at least 60 patients. And, you know, she says: 'That is my minimum. I'll get you 200 [patients] if you like but I am not doing it for anything less than 60' [laughter].*

Certainly, such stances can be motivated by the greedy attitude of some physician-investigators. However, it is important to point out that for many research sites (and especially those organized as specialized research centres), accessing payments from the trials industry may become a matter of survival. For example, this is the declaration of a pharmacologist based in a research centre of a state hospital in Johannesburg:

> *Our main business is clinical trials, so our finances also depend on ... If we are allowed to get 60 patients, it is very beneficial for us to actually get 60 patients. We won't go and enrol patients that fall outside the inclusion and exclusion [criteria[14]] but then, once we know that the study has been submitted for our site, we will already start planning, like ask the nurses at the clinics to start identifying patients for this potential study ... So we plan, so that when we may initiate [the recruitment], then we can get patients as soon as possible.*

As a Research Coordinator of a hospital in Porto Alegre explained, big trials may turn into important funding sources for hospitals:

> *Several bodies, several institutions make clinical research be an important source of [economic] resources. Because all the studies pay well, they pay as well as private activities in big institutions. So almost all institutions wish to capture clinical protocols to be undertaken there because the hospital costs are paid above the average they receive from health insurance schemes and of course the SUS.[15] So it is ... important*

---

14 On inclusion and exclusion criteria, see section 3.4.
15 SUS is the Portuguese acronym for General Health System (*Sistema Único de Saúde*), the governmental, universal health system of Brazil.

for the institution, for its funding, to capture clinical trials' patients, from clinical studies.

Not surprisingly, then, the administrators of some hospitals or chairs of medical departments, willing to 'volunteer' for clinical trials, submit proposals to CROs, pointing out the number of patients served by the prospective site.

Another aspect to take into account is the productivity concerns of some physicians. In certain cases (depending on the source agreements made at the beginning of a study[16]), the company will allow the names of high recruiters to appear in the trial's final publications. At hospitals and universities where the pressure for 'scientific productivity' has risen, this opportunity can be of decisive importance. The following comes from an interview with a physician in Johannesburg:

> *I think it [industrial clinical research] helped us in the sense that we got more familiar with certain medications and so on, and at the end of it all, sometimes, if you're lucky and if you put enough patients onto the study, your name gets put onto a research publication as well. So it did help us in terms of our publication numbers, you know.*

In this way, the 'research productivity' of the trials industry is combined with the 'scientific productivity' of some physicians.

As a CRO's Director of Clinical Teams told me in São Paulo, the division of the *n* among different countries is frequently decided upon by the trial's global management, which is based either in Europe or the United States. At this moment the political dimension of trials is manifested, because the ability to enrol many people for a study leads to an increasing prestige for the investigator and the hospital; the access to economic resources through payments made to investigators; and the provision of innovative therapies to a population of patients that may be the only one to use the medication for a couple of years; among other practical consequences. Therefore, the global distribution of the *n*, instead of being a mere technical decision, determines the fate of hospitals, cities and even whole countries. In order to satisfy 'the number-hungry research industry' (Jonas 1969, p. 235), hospitals have to equip themselves both in terms of medical infrastructures and human skills, as it is shown in the next two sections.

---

16   On source agreements, see section 1.3.

1.6 Multicentre Trials and 'Systems of Objects'

In the same way that research protocols have exclusion criteria,[17] the requisites of studies can often lead to the exclusion of hospitals. Failing to meet the standards of a trial in terms of physical infrastructure, for example, may be a reason why hospitals do not join some studies. This is, for instance, the account of a co-investigator based in hospital in Paris:

> We don't have a very big structure ... because we have only six beds, and these beds are occupied by other studies. And we cannot provide the companies with the 30 beds during 15 days, which they need to run, as they currently run, very intense, quick studies. There is a mismatch between the demands of the industry and our structure.

Another example is the lack of informational tools that ensure the rapid gathering of data, according to the new trends of global research.

As shown in the previous section, a decisive reason why the trials industry looks for hospitals and clinics is quick access to patients, more likely to be achieved when the hospital's large size comes in tandem with its specialization. In a cardiologic hospital in São Paulo, for instance, a Clinical Research Director pointed out the advantages of a specialized institution. The interviewee concluded: 'If [the recruitment] is extremely difficult, there is no problem, because the amount [of patients] is very big. He [the physician] doesn't get the patients today but he'll get them tomorrow.'

Medical infrastructure is a matter of paramount importance for the industry. By locating their activities in hospitals and medical practices, global companies access equipments and tools without which trials cannot be undertaken. Moreover, hospitals can be seen as smoothly running medical machines, for the connections between their specialized sections take place in a simple way. The Research Coordinator of an oncologic practice in São Paulo explained this point. According to her, the practice receives up to 20 research proposals a year, most of which must be refused because some studies demand too sophisticated medical infrastructures:

> So those studies which are more complex, have more procedures and test a strong drug are more difficult to be accepted ... The clinical

---

17 See section 3.4.

research centre of the hospital I used to work for[18] doesn't have this difficulty because it is inside a hospital. So establishing an agreement with the imaging department, with the laboratory, with the anatomy-pathological department, is much easier because they are within the same institution. So it is a conversation between sections ... Because when you establish an agreement with the study's sponsor, you're establishing only one agreement between the study's sponsor and one health institution. In the case of our centre, I would have to establish an agreement with a laboratory, with a unit of intensive care, with a hospital ... So I would have to sign various contracts and control many things for a single study. And sometimes, depending on the amount we receive in order to conduct the study, this is not worth doing.

Thus big and well-equipped hospitals are attractive for the trials industry because of the simple connection among their sections, departments or services. Furthermore, the big hospital seems to be a special environment for studies demanding sophisticated procedures. For example, many studies on Alzheimer's disease require the presence of equipment for magnetic resonance imaging or PET (positron emission tomography) scans, which are expensive devices found only in a small number of hospitals offering tertiary services.

Searching for a putative economic dynamism, some national agencies have decided to attract the trials industry by means of infrastructural improvements. In the UK, for instance, industrial trials have been multiplying in the so-called research units or facilities, whose creation derives from investments mainly made by the National Institutes of Health. In Brazil, the National Network of Clinical Research (*Rede Nacional de Pesquisa Clínica*), an initiative of the Ministry of Health and some national funding agencies, was launched in 2005. Investments enabled to install sophisticated research facilities in some hospitals, and certain research teams decided to work almost exclusively with the trials industry. In a key Brazilian hospital that belongs to this network, investigators, nurses and research coordinators share an investigational area. However, the research unit has no institutional coherence; it is only the location in which many research teams operate, each of them exploring its therapeutic domain and being completely unaware of their counterparts' experiences. In order to know what is really going on in the unit as a whole, it would be unhelpful to ask a trial coordinator or a principal investigator; a monitor working for a CRO would have a more comprehensive notion.

---

18   One of the key private hospitals in São Paulo.

As I claimed elsewhere (Bicudo 2011), the need for good research infrastructure is one factor limiting the geographical flexibility of the trials industry, which frequently depends on its association with certain hospitals. Due to the high sophistication of contemporary trials, the *mediational action* (which provides linkages between the *instrumental* and *communicational rationalities*) cannot be realized without a set of equipments and tools. In Santos (2000a) terms, the trials industry must mobilize many 'systems of objects' (equipments and physical structures) in order to reach targets and meet deadlines.

However, some small medical practices have also become relevant because they can compensate for their modest size by means of their expertise and specialization, which sometimes leads big hospitals to refer patients to them. Small practices can also favour a closer contact between the patient and the medical staff, a circumstance that may facilitate the recruitment of subjects. Indeed, the role played by the medical staff is another crucial factor to be considered by the trials industry, as we see in the following section.

1.7 Multicentre Trials and 'Systems of Actions'

Using Santos (2000a) concepts again, the trials industry searches not only for 'systems of objects' but also 'systems of actions' (human skills, activities and relationships). It needs to find a highly skilled staff that is able to conduct the studies' procedures. On this point, it is interesting to consider the case of French hospitals, where the so-called Centres for Clinical Investigation (*Centres d'Investigation Clinique, CICs*) have appeared since 1992.

Those Centres derived from a partnership between the National Institute for Medical Health and Research (Inserm) and the Public Assistance, which manages the hospitals of Paris. Gradually, CICs have appeared in many other French cities and especially in hospitals attached to key universities. D'Enfert and colleagues (2003, p. 289) are right to affirm that: 'Centres for Clinical Investigation (CICs) ... are a good example of structures that favour the conduct of projects within an optimal scientific and logistical environment.' These centres aim to enhance the links between basic research and medical practice, thereby fostering efforts that were described as a move 'from the bench to the bedside' (Wainwright, Williams et al. 2006). Both academic studies and industrial trials can be conducted in CICs, some of which favour the work with the industry. In Table 1.1, some data is presented about the staff of three CICs I visited during my fieldwork in Paris.

Table 1.1   **The research staff of three CICs in Paris**

Foundation of the CIC	Staff						
	Physicians	Nurses	Pharmacologists and pharmacists	Technicians	Secretaries	Others*	Total
Until 1995	3	4	1	0	1	1	**10**
Until 1995	4	5	1	1	1	1	**13**
After 2000	2	6	0	2	1	5	**16**

*   Administrators, laboratory specialists, social workers, administrative assistants and clinical research advisers.
Source: Fieldwork.

As Table 1.1 above illustrates, the range of professionals involved in clinical trials has been expanding. Nowadays, the industry can even mobilize professionals such as lawyers, software developers or data managers.

To be sure, 'classical roles' continue to be crucial for the conduct of trials, as is the case for nurses. It would suffice to say that what Mueller wrote in 1997 is still valid: 'nurses, rather than physician-investigators, are directly engaged with trial protocols ... they have the most frequent and sustained contact with patient-volunteers (1997, p. 63)'. However, such classical roles must nowadays be played in very different environments. Nurses may have to deal with sophisticated standards and tools such as electronic data forms. That is why, in many sites, they have to undergo specific training. A physician based in a French CIC told me 'When it comes to nurses, when they arrive to our service, in the first year they have part of their time free to do courses on clinical research.'

If one analyses the historical evolution of clinical trials, the position of research coordinator is the most important role that has been created in recent years. Research coordinators deal with various aspects of trials, from the organization of the study's data to the regulatory process that every trial must undergo. As physicians and nurses become busier and busier, coordinators are the ones who fill the professional voids of clinical trials.

Finally and obviously, physicians are decisive actors in global trials, and not only because they play the role of principal investigators (PIs). Contacting them can multiply the advantages of the trials industry, insofar as physicians frequently work in more than one hospital. Thus they are able to choose the best location for a trial, mobilizing other professionals to run the study at these settings.

Principal investigators, in spite of this grand title, do not play a very crucial role in the conduct of clinical trials. Many physicians participate in several trials at the same time, although their actual participation may be limited to bureaucratically signing some forms (Mueller 1997; Fisher 2009). In Johannesburg, for example, I visited a research centre that is linked to a university. This centre has a partnership with two hospitals in the city, from which some physicians are recruited to work as principal investigators. For these physicians it is not even necessary to visit the clinical centre; they only need to sign contracts and see research subjects from time to time in order to comply with the study's procedures, whereas numerous and decisive study tasks are conducted by nurses and research coordinators based in the research centre.

Thus in the everyday work of global trials, principal investigators tend to become 'ancillary investigators'. Reinforcing this event, as Vallejo (2006, p. 190) noted, in every trial about a third of the investigators are new to the enterprise. Thus, because pharma companies and CROs are always approaching new physicians, the trials industry seems to be testing not only drugs but also investigators and sites.

When it comes to sites, those which belong to universities acquire a special worth because the prestige of respected universities can be used by the industry to convey the 'scientific purposes' of multicentre trials. Indeed, I interviewed 17 principal investigators in my fieldwork, all of whom were attached to a university.

According to the *theory of communicative action*, human activities are not simply undertaken: they are also *expressed* and *justified* to other social actors (Habermas 2008). The trials industry, in addition to conducting its activities, has to present them as desirable, serious and relevant operations. A strategy toward the construction of such *discourse* is precisely the suggestion that multicentre trials have to do with a global research effort. Thus as long as physicians assure the presence of important academic and medical 'brands' in global research, their slight commitment will be of no concern to CROs and pharma companies. Sismondo (2009) showed that from the outset of a clinical study sponsors must set up a publication plan, which involves the inclusion of articles in key scientific journals. The recruitment of eminent physicians and universities for clinical studies belongs to this same effort to cover global research with a 'scientific layer'.

Because physicians are too busy to work on their own, within a hospital many research teams are to be found, whose size depends on the size of the study (number of patients to be recruited). Depending on the institution, a research team can be composed of dozens of professionals. For example, in Paris I interviewed a physician in whose research team 15 people were working, including statisticians, coordinators, technicians and health economists. In a cardiologic hospital in São Paulo, I interviewed one of the Research Coordinators of the angioplasty section. In her research team, in addition to the main investigator, studies can involve up to ten other physicians who play the role of co-investigators.

Research teams were first created in order to help busy principal investigators. Nowadays, however, some nurses and coordinators seem to be as busy as their research bosses. The expansion of trials in hospitals might suggest a beneficial development in medical projects. However, it is important to consider that global research is shaping the organization of hospitals in unexpected ways. For instance, in many hospitals, multicentre trials have increased the workload of an already overburdened staff and expanded the use of already highly required equipments. In São Paulo, a Director for Clinical Management talked about saturation:

> *So in Brazil the biggest hub of clinical research is São Paulo, isn't it?*
>
> *Yes, yes, yes … But what are we observing, Edison? … Everything is rather … how can I say … saturated. Saturated. There are several other CROs like us, there are pharmaceutical companies that run studies directly. So those centres that are more targeted, you know, face difficulties to do it, both in terms of staff to conduct research and patients.*

This trend is likely to be reinforced because many hospitals tend to increase their research efforts through the establishment of partnerships with CROs.

1.8 Recruitment Partnerships

The relationship between the trials industry and some hospitals has reached a state of *entanglement*. On the one hand, companies rely on those particular sites to conduct their most strategic studies, especially those demanding large numbers of research subjects. On the other hand, those hospitals frame industrial trials as an ordinary part of their operations, having become used to placing various resources (professionals, equipments, rooms or even whole buildings) at the global companies' disposal.

Basically, it is possible to point to three kinds of partnerships. The first and most frequent relation is established between a CRO and a physician. In this way, the company would always offer its trials to some investigators, particularly those who are key opinion leaders[19] or good recruiters. Second, the partnership can involve a department within a hospital. This arrangement would be more frequent when the physicians of the department are more welcoming to industrial trials; there are professionals to help investigators; the department works with diseases that are commonly targeted by the industry (such as cancer or cardiovascular diseases); or the department's research infrastructure fits the trials industry's standards. Finally, there is a small number of cases in which the partnership involves the hospital as a whole. Generally, such agreements involve big, pivotal hospitals focusing on particular therapeutic domains.

In a general way, CROs glean two advantages from the establishment of partnerships. The first is rapid access to physicians and their patient populations. In some agreements, the company can achieve relationships with all the physicians based in a hospital quite quickly. By sending letters or forms to them, it is possible to identify those who are interested in industrial research. In this way, CROs have access to important investigator 'armies', which can be subsequently trained with courses on clinical, regulatory or technical aspects of trials. In some occasions, the company may also provide the site with a Recruitment Manager to help the hospital's staff in some studies.

The second benefit enjoyed by CROs that have partnerships with many hospitals is access to different regions of a country. This is important because some diseases can have higher levels of occurrence in some areas than others. A multinational CRO, for example, has established many partnerships in France, thereby having quick access to hospitals and investigators in cities like Paris, Marseille, Nancy and Amiens. The same phenomenon takes place at the

---

19   On key opinion leaders, see section 3.1.

global scale. The company has partnerships with huge hospitals in many cities across the world such as London, Pretoria, Washington and São Paulo. CROs will be more willing to partner institutions that display very high recruitment performance and are able to put many hundreds of patients into clinical trials every year.

The main implication of a partnership, whether it involves physicians, departments or whole hospitals, is preferred participation in the CRO's trials. Thus, whenever a new study is initiated, the company will offer it to its partners in the first place. As a Site Manager who is based in Paris told me:

It is indeed very important for us to be able to include into a project the biggest number of partners which is possible, in order for these centres to include many patients or many more patients than the non-partner sites. Recruitment partnerships can derive from simple conversations or involve the signature of written documents. In all the cases we are dealing with negotiations that escape the domain of *institutions* and the law. In fact, even though they may bring interesting economic resources to some hospitals, as well as medical benefits to physicians and patients, these partnerships are always the product of individual companies' and sites' decisions. We are dealing with *implicit* agreements whereby crucial players involved (basically the state and patients) do not have any say in the whole process. As a result of these close relations between some hospitals and the trials industry, *entanglements* have been created in which companies' operations mingle with state-owned sites' features, a phenomenon that is analysed in the next section.

1.9 The Indirect Privatization of Hospitals

In an interview in Madrid, a CRO's Director for Site Identification used a curious expression:

> *It is the first time I hear the expression 'semi-private hospitals.'*
> *What are semi-private hospitals?*
>
> *Let's see. Semi-private. Some hospitals have ... They are public but they have, so to speak, separate funding ... How can I say. In the case of Spain, for instance, you can have a hospital which is public but there is a Foundation ... And these Foundations, if they are based on investigation,*

receive some money to support part of the department's activities ...
they are supporting research with a further funding source.[20]

While providing this cautious explanation, the interviewee had in mind the case of Research Foundations, which are becoming very common in Spain and other countries. Although he was not precise in framing those organizations as 'semi-private', his point of view and the classification he used are not illogical. Actually, things are 'complicated to understand, even for us, because it is a relatively new thing', as a CRO's Contract Specialist put it in an interview in São Paulo. She was also talking about Research Foundations, which, from her point of view, can be framed as 'a public body but with private administration', which is not a completely accurate description either. These 'minor mistakes' are understandable because, as we shall see,[21] Foundations deal with private funding spent in state hospitals, thereby suggesting strange blends.

If it is better to be cautious when it comes to classifying Research Foundations, there are many other situations in which the close association between state hospitals and the trials industry is more than clear. Some examples have become famous and almost classic, such as the friendly relationships between the pharmaceutical industry and some physicians who may, for instance, work as pharma companies advisors. Of the seventeen principal investigators I interviewed, six (one in the UK, one in Spain, two in France, one in Brazil, and one in South Africa) declared they had had or were having experience as advisors.

Another well-known example is the installation, by the trials industry, of relatively simple equipments, which are kept by the site on completion of the study. A Managing Director of a South African CRO told me: 'If you're starting a new site like in Africa, very often the pharma companies will provide the infrastructure and then you train up the investigator.' In some rare cases, the trials industry may promote quite generous improvements in a hospital's infrastructure, especially in its most common partner sites. According to a Research Coordinator who works in a big state hospital in London:

The one good thing about commercial companies though ... is that they
donate things that are really, really valuable to us for research, like MRI
[magnetic resonance imaging] machines or space, they build us space

---

20 'Semi-private' was also the classification chosen by a French Director for Site Initiation when she spoke of the oncologic sites with which the CRO often works.

21 Section 2.1.

to use for research, labs and things like that. So this is a great thing ...
Commercial companies donate 50, 60, 70 thousand pounds to a P.I. for
him to use it however he need it in order to run his studies.

Here, things depend on the way we look at them and the words we choose
to describe them. In fact, such 'donations' might also be considered as sheer
commercial investment.

Parallel to the installation of equipments and tools, some hospitals may
have whole agencies or units of companies nested within their buildings.
That is the case of a private recruitment centre I visited in London, which is
physically attached to key hospitals in some British cities. Another example
comes from São Paulo, where I visited a clinical trials company that was born
inside a state hospital, having spent almost ten years there.

In Cape Town, another company is still there, occupying some space on
two floors of a state hospital, where it has operated for 11 years. Physicians
are hired from private practices to play the role of P.I. and identify subjects,
whereas about 30 per cent of those subjects come from the hospital itself. I
interviewed the owner and director of this company who, in a very cautious,
almost mysterious vein, spoke of the enterprise and defined it as follows: 'we
work in dedicated areas within the hospital but it is not part of the hospital. We
are a private unit.' Thus, a Brazilian Site Manager based in a CRO was correct
when she told me: 'There are private sites within public institutions.'

Nowadays, some hospitals and the trials industry are forming a coherent
mixture that is difficult to disentangle. In many countries, state hospitals are
the main sites used by CROs. In European countries with a strong health
system, such as the UK, Spain and France, state hospitals can be even more
strategic. In France, for instance, 87 per cent of the investigators registered in a
multinational CRO's database in 2010 were based in state hospitals. Working
with these sites the trials industry may have its costs reduced, for as a Spanish
Site Initiation Leader explained to me: 'Often, in public institutions, in public
centres, the costs of radiologic tests are smaller.' At the same time, state
hospitals, as opposed to private ones, hold more 'investigational experience',
as a Spanish Clinical Manager put it.

One of the consequences of the expanding number of multicentre trials is
the potential reduction in the number of academic studies in state institutions,
especially in those research teams, departments or hospitals which are more

oriented toward industrial research. The process is subtle and very difficult to grasp but it was possible to gather some information in my fieldwork. Table 1.2 is a draft and tentative effort towards the depiction of this phenomenon.

Table 1.2   Proportion of industrial studies developed in state hospitals, according to type of health care unit

Type	City	Research staff*	Reference	Approximate proportion of industrial trials (%)
Private company within a hospital	Cape Town	30	June 2011	95.0
Research team within a hospital	São Paulo	4	March 2011	80.0
	Porto Alegre	5	Annual average	95.0
Department within a hospital	Paris	15	Annual average	50.0
Clinical trials unit within a hospital	Paris	13	Annual average	20.0
	Paris	150	Annual average	30.0
	Paris	9	November 2010	77.1
Institute within a hospital complex	São Paulo	?	Annual average	17.6
Cluster of hospitals	London	?	February 2011	25.0
	London	?	February 2011	33.3
	Porto Alegre	?	Annual average	98.0

*   Here I am including people working only with clinical research and whose activities, therefore, are not related to official health care. Thus, the principal investigator him or herself is not included here. For the categories of 'Institutes' and 'Clusters', this number could not be obtained because it would be necessary to talk to all the investigators of the institution in order to know if they have research teams or even private clinical research companies.
Source: interviews conducted in fieldwork.

Some sites seem to be rather academic-driven, as is the case of the French clinical research unit which, in spite of its high number of investigators (more than 150), has only 30 per cent of its studies sponsored by the trials industry, in the annual average. However, there can also be examples such as the research team based in a hospital in São Paulo, which, in March 2011, was working with the industry in about 80 per cent of its trials. This means that some institutions may have research programmes that are largely dependent on the global industry's choices.

Despite of its limitations, Table 1.2 suggests a trend. The more clinical trials escape the control of individual research teams and fall into the management sphere of large *institutions*, the smaller the proportion of industrial trials. This phenomenon might be reflecting the steering force that comes into play when negotiations emerge into the *institutional* domain. Indeed, the last row of the table depicts an atypical situation, for those hospitals have not yet established an effective control over clinical research, as many of its Brazilian counterparts have.

The proliferation of industrial studies may therefore have a crucial impact on the sites' research pathways. It is known, for instance, that oncology has been one of the main therapeutic areas targeted by pharma companies (Seruga et al. 2010). In my fieldwork, I identified many examples of efforts being made, and resources being invested, in the area of cancer studies. Considering the entrepreneurial choices underpinning such 'oncologic adventure', it is worth asking if cancer has indeed become a 'word's high problem' or it is simply 'highly problematized by world companies'. Whereas oncologic trials continue to display a steady expansion, some other diseases may turn into less strategic fields, depending on economic and scientific scenarios. As one Research Coordinator based in a hospital in Madrid told me:

> There are many times in which there is much investigational development in a certain disease, like lymphoma, so there are many studies, because many new molecules are launched ... Right now there are many studies on multiple myelomas because they have been intensely investigated, whereas other diseases remain a bit more at margin and have only three or four studies.

Therefore, the trials industry is determining research pathways to be taken by certain medical institutions, which are increasingly playing the role of research sites. The initiation of dozens of studies on a certain disease, the mobilization of hundreds of caregivers in several countries and the subsequent recruitment of thousands of patients all over the world derive from technical decisions taken in the headquarters of global companies whose staff may be lacking appropriate knowledge about national needs and features.

To be sure, some shifts that may be brought about by the trials industry can be beneficial for many state hospitals in certain ways. By running multicentre trials, they can learn sophisticated scientific procedures and streamline their (sometimes too bureaucratic) methods. However, if such crucial changes are to happen in state hospitals, where most people look for health care, then it is important that the process is discussed in *explicit* forums. Abandoned to *implicit* arenas, as it currently is, this process is steered either by the concerns of a handful of individuals or the powerful actions of the trials industry. In a hospital in Porto Alegre, for instance, a Research Coordinator explained to me how clinical research has evolved within the site over the last years. He started his account by remembering that clinical trials first appeared in the hospital in the 1980s:

> *And the institution was not prepared to do it ... It did not have this tradition. It had no tradition in learning and doing research. Basically, it provided health care. This situation made researchers induce the institution to create spaces to underpin clinical research administratively. The institution didn't encourage the researchers. It was the researchers that came over and said: 'Look, we need to do it, we need an ethics committee, we need a place to register these things, we need a registered laboratory, we need certified infrastructure.' They started demanding those things. As the institution has never aimed to have research as a source of resources, or at least an organized source of work, there has never been interest in putting a structure at the researchers' disposal, including social workers, pharmacists, nurses, technicians, to conduct research on behalf of the institution.*

Arguably, some interpreters would frame this initiative as scientific bravery, especially if we consider that the interviewee was talking about a small group of researchers that barely represented 2 per cent of the hospital's medical population. However, it is important to ponder what the scientific future of a country can be if its research policies continue to depend on a few investigators' will. The situation becomes even trickier if we imagine that such small groups can have their demands supported (or even instilled) by the trials industry itself.

Slowly, the control over research activities undertaken in hospitals slips from the hands of national agencies. The main beneficiaries of this process are the companies composing the trials industry, which become able to mandate rhythms of work, research pathways, deadlines, procedures and many other things. The example of multicentre trials teaches us, then, that it is not necessary for national states to formally hand over an activity to private companies in order to privatize it. Even though hospitals, framed as research settings, continue to be owned by the state, they are escaping the state's control in order to be indirectly ruled by powerful multinational companies.

The putatively homogeneous space in which the multinational industry operates comes to be extended to sites themselves. In this process, *mediational actions* (carried out in hospitals by the medical staff) play a central role, for its inputs enable *instrumental actors* to identify opportunities and targets for the establishment of new standards. The process is further intensified by the monetary aspects of trials, which ask for more controllability, institutional arrangements and complex agreements, as analysed in the next chapter.

2

Payments: Global Trials and Local Agreements

In the previous chapter, we explored the impacts of global trials on the organization of hospitals, focusing, particularly, on infrastructures, human resources and rhythms of work. In addition to these processes, there must be changes in terms of rules, guidelines and institutional instruments. As I claimed elsewhere (Bicudo 2006), standards are nowadays the driving force in the configuration of geographical territories. As research sites, hospitals cannot escape this process and, consequently, have to undergo a whole set of institutional renewals in order to adjust to global standards. Moreover, as claimed before, a new rationality needs to be installed in hospitals. Certainly, the creation of new institutional arrangements and rules enhances this installation, for as Luhmann (1983) teaches us, standards and rules serve, primarily, to spread rationales and expectations.

Nevertheless, we are not dealing with a completely rigid and standardized activity in which all procedures are fixed at the outset. 'The problem with clinical trials is that we cannot talk about a general functioning because things vary. Each site is different. You never know what you're going to find', as conveyed by a CRO's monitor, somebody whose job consists of visiting sites and trying to enforce global procedures. Thus it is crucial to point out that the complex realm of standards and directives that shape clinical research is complemented by a large set of uncertain negotiations and flexible schemes.

Studying the institutional and regulatory configuration of hospitals involved in global trials, as well as the obscure realm of negotiations and agreements, is important not only to understand what happens in particular institutions but, mainly, to verify whether such configuration has been changed in *democratic* or *conspiratorial* ways. In order to undertake this analysis, we shall focus, first, on the creation, within hospitals, of new agencies and offices to deal with global clinical studies. Then, we move on to addressing the financial aspects of trials, starting with the issues of research contracts and budgets. Subsequently, we analyse the pathways followed by the payments made by the trials industry. This analysis is followed by an exploration of a new type of (hybrid) work that has appeared in state hospitals. Finally, we draw attention to hidden agreements carried out in the universe of global trials.

2.1 Institutional Mechanisms

In 2008, the administrators of some public hospitals located in a French southern city decided that it was time to foster clinical research. Helped by the city's Chamber of Commerce, they prepared a presentation that was sent to the global headquarters of a CRO in the United States. The company rapidly became interested in the partnership, which would involve important university hospitals and more than 50 investigators willing to take part in clinical trials. After a quick process of negotiations, the partnership was signed and these hospitals, which were conducting 8 studies with the CRO in 2008, had 38 trials in 2011.

To be sure, this expansion cannot be reached without important adjustments made by the medical site, which must prepare itself for the arrival of the *instrumental rationality* of global companies. One of the most decisive adjustments to be made has to do with the financial management of clinical trials. Theoretically, state hospitals can only receive and manage funding from government sources. In order to circumvent this barrier, hospitals have created some structures that enable them to look for alternative funding and receive payments from private companies.

In Spain, the solution found by hospital administrators has been the use of the so-called Research Foundation (*Fundación para la Investigación*). Generally, these Foundations are able to deal with many types of scientific investigation but in recent years they have focused on industrial clinical trials. Foundations are useful because they can receive and manage funding from both government and private sources, subsequently allocating these resources for research activities carried out in the institution.

Nowadays, the most important Spanish hospitals have their own Research Foundation. Depending on the stance of administrators and the agreements made by physician-investigators, the Foundation can either stress academic activities or operate more in tune with the trials industry. Spanish state hospitals, which are the most important clinical sites in the country, have become capable of assimilating global trials and keeping track of the monetary flows of studies. A similar arrangement can be verified in Brazil, where many hospitals are also endowed with Foundations (*Fundações*), and, much more rarely, in South Africa, where one finds the so-called Consortiums.

In the UK, hospitals have spawned Research and Development (R&D) Offices, which also deal with financial and regulatory aspects of clinical trials. As the biggest British hospitals are linked to universities, the R&D Office ends up having a mixed composition, because their staff can be hired by either the trust[1] or the college. As was the case of Spanish Foundations, British R&D Offices have taken over activities that were previously controlled by individual investigators. According to a Director for Site Management interviewed in London:

> *Ten, fifteen years ago it was different but all contracts now are signed by R&D [the R&D office] rather than by the investigator, and money is paid to the R&D fund rather than to the investigator. It is now up to the R&D to distribute [such resources] accordingly within the hospital. Because some money may need to go to pharmacy, some to radiology, etcetera etcetera.*

R&D Offices have proven so helpful that even small hospitals, lacking resources to build up their own structures, are using the so-called Service-level Agreements, by means of which a small hospital can hire services from an R&D Office installed in a bigger hospital.

The institutional solution found in France has a different nature. In the past, the legal management of clinical studies was undertaken at a regional scale, for in France regions also play a fundamental administrative role. However, as the regulatory aspects of trials have become more and more complex, it was seen that this management needed to be done on a smaller, and therefore more accurate, scale. The Public Assistance of Paris created the so-called Units of Clinical Research (*Unités de Recherche Clinique, URCs*) whose tasks involve the financial and regulatory control of clinical trials undertaken in university hospitals. Differently from other countries, URCs can, and often do, comprise more than one hospital. Moreover, URCs often work in close association with

---

1   Trusts are public sector corporations providing services on behalf of the UK's National Health Services (NHS).

CICs,[2] sometimes sharing physical locations and staff with them. Today the city of Paris holds 12 URCs.

Thus some institutional engineering must take place, because relationships between state hospitals and private companies do not work without some institutional adjustments.[3] As we have seen, one of the main reasons why these changes are necessary is the inflow of 'private money' into state hospitals. In addition to managing the monetary part of protocols, and therefore freeing PIs from this task, Foundations and Offices can also provide some advice on financial matters. That is what is being done by the Foundation of a hospital in São Paulo, which created a centre whose goal is to organize the budgetary and bureaucratic tasks of trials. According to a physician-investigator I interviewed:

> The centre has people with some expertise in the budgetary analysis of projects with both funding from the industry and other kinds of funding. So we can go there to discuss: 'Look, this is the budget of a study I was given or I want to do or I want to propose. Is it suitable or not?' They give us much help with all the contractual part, you know, when you have contracts with the industry, or even with the regulatory part.

> **And is this contractual part still complicated?**

> It was more complicated in the past. I think now we have a pathway within the hospital, which was created by the centre itself. It is a very clear pathway for the procedures of clinical research ... It instructed the researchers very much. Very, very much.

Thus, promoting more institutional control in global trials does not amount to depriving investigators of their previous scientific freedom. In addition to giving coherence to the relations between physicians and the trials industry, such institutional schemes can help investigators understand the tricky matters of global research.

Payments made by the industry can reach important amounts compared to the sometimes scarce investments that hospitals get from state agencies. In order to normalize and control their occurrence, the trials industry and medical

---

2   On the French CICs, see section 1.7.
3   In the case of some hospitals and clinics, the payments of clinical studies continue to be received and managed through individual agreements, an issue that is explored in section 2.5.

institutions have used a tool called research contract, a normative form that we analyse in the next section.

2.2 What is a Research Contract?

Within a clinical study, a formal relationship is established between the sponsor, the CRO, the site and the staff responsible for the clinical procedures to be undertaken. If something goes amiss during the process, there are legal responsibilities to be invoked. In addition, practical and economic commitments have to be made. In order to govern all of these matters, the parties involved sign the so-called research contract, which is the main legal document framing a global trial. As a Contract Specialist told me: 'Without a contract, there is no research.'

According to Serrano and Grau (2006), contracts deal with issues such as costs of the study, reimbursements to patients, and expenses with equipments. Therefore, the signature of this document is a pivotal issue for CROs, especially because by means of previous agreements between them and pharma companies, they act as the sponsors' legal representatives. In most cases, when a pharma company transfers the conduct of a study to a CRO, only the latter will sign the research contract, even though the major legal responsibility continues to belong to the pharma company. In addition, research contracts are important because, depending on local circumstances 'the signature of the contract is what provokes the biggest delays in the beginning of the trial', as Serrano and Grau (2006, p. 151) explained.

As clinical studies have become more and more sophisticated, research contracts themselves have turned into very complex and detailed documents. According to a Spanish Site Initiation Leader, they used to be quite simple, stating only financial issues and monetary values; gradually, sponsors realized that by means of such documents they could acquire legal protection: contracts have thus been amplified and gained numerous sections. In a hospital in London, a Research Coordinator showed me, on the screen of her computer, a 41-page-long Word document, which was actually a research contract involving the trust and a biotech company.

Nowadays, there are three main issues to be addressed by contracts: the confidentiality of all the parties involved; intellectual property; and procedures and rights pertaining to the publication of the study's results. Financial matters continue to be a key section but the relative space they occupy in a contract has been drastically reduced. Indeed, costs, payments and reimbursements are now often stated in a single page attached to the main document.

The issue is so central to CROs that many specialists have been formed or hired by those companies in order to deal exclusively with contracts. In the past, the so-called Contract Specialists were quite rare and their operations were undertaken within broader departments. Nowadays, Contract Specialists are an almost obligatory function within a multinational CRO, often gathering in specialized departments and thus solidifying the 'regulatory business' pointed out by McGoey and Jackson (2009, p. 110). For example, the French unit of a CRO manages one of the so-called Initiation Teams, composed of 16 people, 7 of them working exclusively with contracts. Another French office of another CRO also holds the management of a Site Initiation Team composed of 22 employees who deal with ethics committees, regulatory matters and research contracts. Even though these teams are organized internationally,[4] it is important for CROs to have at least one Contract Specialist in key countries so that the company can easily adjust to local rules. Indeed, the contractual process of trials can vary considerably, as a rapid review of our five national situations testifies.

In the interviews I conducted in Spain, many people, based both in CROs and research sites, hastened to say that research contracts are the main factor delaying studies in the country. However, many contracts are signed in two months, a short period compared to some other countries. Generally, contracts are signed by the PI,[5] the institution he or she is based in, and the company. Differently from what happens in many countries, Spanish sites do not accept working with contract templates proposed by the trials industry. Hospitals of the same community have formed agreements in order to elaborate upon their own templates, thereby forming some 'contractual areas', as shown in the following map.

Thus most Spanish communities have created their own templates, which have become mandatory in the work with the trials industry. In October 2010, one of the CROs involved in my study had 80 sites in the white area, 37 in the soft grey area, and 11 sites in the darkest area. Therefore, the existence of a regional template does not seem to represent a major barrier. However, if this

---

4   See section 1.2.
5   P.I. is an acronym for principal investigator, a physician who is the main individual responsible for the study undertaken in a particular site.

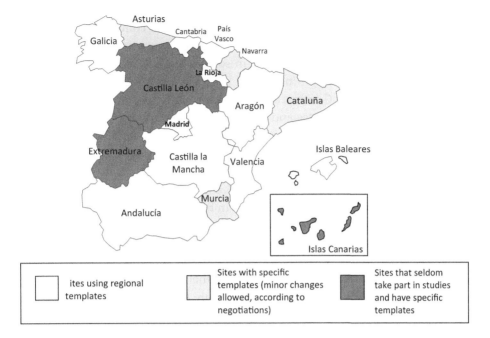

Figure 2.1   Research contract templates in the Spanish Autonomous Communities (*Comunidades Autónomas*), 2011

Source: One of the global CROs that took part in my fieldwork

situation facilitates the process when the trial is conducted in a single region (companies already know all the Spanish templates), it creates problems when it comes to developing trials in many regions. In this case, the industry has to ask for contractual changes in order to address the specificities of the study, which can be difficult, if not impossible, in those regions that are less open to negotiations. Contractual flexibility (that is, the willingness to negotiate some points of the contract) is certainly one of the reasons why this CRO had the biggest number of sites in the region of Cataluña, the quality and organization of medical institutions being another outstanding factor.

France is a country with complex institutional and bureaucratic schemes, and this is also the case for clinical research contracts. Different from the Spanish situation, in France each study requires the signature of two contracts. The first one is called the Hospital Convention and is signed by the company and the hospital. A few years ago the French government, in an initiative supported by the French association of pharma companies (LEEM, *Les enterprises du médicament*), launched a national template which has been increasingly adopted by French hospitals. The second contract involves the company and the PI, and the company's template is commonly used.[6] Sometimes, this contract involves the whole research team but in some situations, which are not very rare, the company must sign individual contracts with every member of the research team. A CRO's Contract Specialist based in Paris remembered a study that involved two French sites and entailed the signature of 14 contracts. With this complex environment, the contractual process takes much longer than in Spain. On average, it takes four months but it can take up to six.

In terms of research contracts, the UK and South Africa have simple and quick processes, but for different reasons. In British hospitals, R&D Offices are responsible for contractual negotiations. Almost repeating the French case, the UK's Department of Health, supported by pharma companies, launched, some years ago, a national template that is being rapidly adopted by research sites. This template seems to be even more detailed than its French counterpart, for it even recommends standardized ways to declare the study's costs, making the process quite rapid. In an R&D office I visited in London, a third of contracts are signed in one month, the total average being three months.

In South Africa, negotiations are seldom overseen by the medical institution. In most cases, the P.I. is the only actor responsible for taking decisions, making choices and signing the contract. In Johannesburg, I interviewed a CRO's Contract Specialist who deals with contracts for both South Africa and the UK. She told me that whereas in the UK the institution carries out about 95 per cent of contract negotiations and the P.I. is the main player in about 5 per cent of cases, in South Africa the opposite occurs. Ironically, the contractual process is amazingly quick here, because of the 'easy-going' stance of South African investigators, as this interviewee defined it. Investigators are keen to accept the companies' templates and seldom ask for changes. In a private clinical trials centre I visited in Cape Town, the contractual process generally takes one week, on average.

Brazil's situation is a mixture of what happens in the UK and South Africa. Indeed, it is possible to say that Brazil is abandoning old traits and moving toward more robust *institutional* structures such as those verified in the UK. Most of the key Brazilian sites have Foundations or Clinical Research Centres to deal with research contracts. However, in some (state and private) hospitals situations remain in which negotiations are carried out by individual investigators. So far

---

6   As explained in section 2.6, this contract frequently involves the investigator's research association.

no contract template has been created in this country, whose government is only beginning to realize the political relevance that clinical research has acquired. Because of this, sites have worked with templates proposed by the industry and formulated their own 'mini-rules' of clinical research. For example, the number of signatures varies from three to five, depending on the site's organization and bureaucratic tendencies. The turnaround time for negotiations also depends on the institution, private hospitals being more rapid than their government counterparts and their heavy bureaucracy.

Certainly, global companies are aware of these national particularities. However, they sometimes still seem to suppose that the 'global arena' is more homogeneous than it really is. In São Paulo, a CRO's Contract Specialist told me, for instance, that some sponsors propose contract templates in which international standards have more weight than the Brazilian regulations, an attitude that generally provokes delays in the negotiation.

The issue of research contracts reveals a *complementary* phenomenon in clinical trials. On the one hand, these contracts have become a juridical form adopted in several countries. On the other hand, they are used in different ways in different countries. In some national situations (particularly the UK and Spain), research contracts are subject to high degrees of *institutionalization*, being negotiated and signed by representatives of the medical institution; whereas in other countries (particularly South Africa) the process continues to be carried out by individual investigators. In all of the countries, however, there are some issues that contracts control precariously, opening up some leeway for *implicit* negotiations between companies and investigators. To begin the analysis of this phenomenon, the issue of research budgets is focused on in the next section.

2.3 What is a Study's Budget?

With payments received from the trials industry, hospitals have to adopt new financial methods. To be precise, 'payment' is not the correct term here, as hospitals are never really 'paid' by companies. The correct word is 'reimbursement', for the trials industry only needs to give the expenses incurred as a consequence of a study's procedures back to hospitals. Just as someone would compensate the depreciation of a machine, the industry reimburses the costs it triggers.

However, the intricacies of the topic start here, for as soon as one talks to people involved in global trials, it becomes clear that in many cases we are not dealing with simple compensation. Generally, reimbursements made by the trials industry are higher than those that would normally be realized. In state hospitals, the surplus between what is reimbursed by the industry and what would normally be compensated by the state is even more substantial. In this way, a sort of 'economic rationale' may emerge whereby people recognize that global trials can indeed be a source of additional funding for hospitals.

It is risky to firmly claim that reimbursements received by hospitals through their participation in global trials reach sky-rocketing amounts, as there are no data available on this topic. In a clinical research centre of a key hospital I visited in Paris, one-fifth of the funding comes from the trials industry, according to a physician who is also the centre's director. Even though we are lacking precise data, two phenomena must be considered. First, from a sociological point of view, the emergence of the aforementioned 'rationale', which leads people to frame trials as a parallel source of funding within hospitals, is more meaningful than the actual financial results brought about by the process. Second, reimbursements from the trials industry, however scant they may be, tend to become a normal part of some hospitals' economic calculations. In São Paulo, a physician who coordinates a clinical research centre of a state hospital told me:

> **But for instance, for the organization of the centre, does this budget that is obtained with industrial studies represent an important financial complement?**
>
> *... Let's see. Here we have a fee that remains from every study in an account of our clinical research centre and with these resources, we manage to generate advancements and equipments that the governmental funding does not generate...*
>
> **So these are strategic resources?**
>
> *These are resources ... Let's say, it is not a huge amount but it helps us a bit in the management of the centre.*

Reimbursements to hospitals, as well as payments to investigators and research teams, must be stated in the research contract, generally in an attachment to the main document. This is the study's budget, in which the sponsor must declare two main values: the amounts to be provided per procedure and per patient in order to reimburse the hospital costs; and the payments to be made to the investigator and his or her team as remuneration for their work. Frequently, what the budget states is not what the hospital and the team really get, as some procedures and visits to the site may be added or dropped during the trial. However, the study's budget must serve as a fair estimation about the study's monetary flows.

When the hospital possesses something like a Research Foundation or an R&D Office,[7] this body receives the two elements of a study's budget (reimbursements to the hospital and payments to investigators). When it comes to payments to the medical staff, the Foundation or Office will retain part of them in order to meet its own costs and pay its own staff. The proportion that is taken by the managing body (frequently called 'overhead') is subject to huge variation depending on the country and the institution. During my fieldwork, for example, I came across a Brazilian Foundation that retains 6.5 per cent of payments; a Spanish Foundation keeping 20.0 per cent; and another Brazilian Foundation whose overhead amounts to 60.0 per cent.

Therefore, the payments and reimbursements made by the trials industry within a study generally follow the pathways depicted in Figure 2.2.

Reimbursements are simply transferred to the hospital's services (radiology, laboratories, imaging, among others). From the payment to the research team, the Foundation retains its overhead. It can also form a 'research fund' so that researchers and students based in the hospital can apply for financial support to conduct academic or medical studies. The biggest part of payments is reserved for the research team conducting the trial for the industry. However, even though the team, or more frequently the PI, can decide on how the money is to be used (buying equipments, hiring professionals, funding participations in conferences and so on), there is no direct access to these resources, which are kept by the Foundation in a so-called 'research account'. In order for these resources to be spent, the team needs to inform the Foundation, which will then realize the indicated expense, making sure that resources are destined for research activities.[8]

---

7   See section 2.1.
8   In some sites, investigators are allowed to receive some payment as part of their personal salaries. This is what happens, for instance, in a Porto Alegre private university, as the Coordinator of its Technological Agency explained to me.

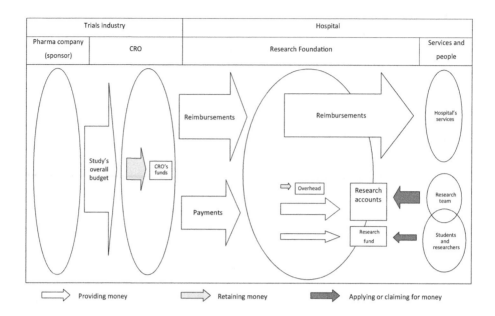

Figure 2.2   Typical monetary pathways in a global clinical trial
Source: created by the author with information from the fieldwork and literature

The monetary pathways schematized in Figure 2.2 are slowly being normalized into the life of hospitals, strengthening the steering role of *institutions*. In addition to being a clear system, its elements can be stated and ruled by a research contract. It was probably with similar systems in mind that Serrano and Grau (2006, p. 150) wrote: 'All the economic aspects pertaining to the clinical trial must be reflected in a contract between the sponsor and each of the sites where the trial is to be realized.'

Thus it is crucial to highlight the role played by *institutions*, which can be sociologically defined as sets of behaviours or procedures that come to be consolidated and normalized within a social group. *Institutions* can derive both from traditions (such as the institution of marriage) or from the mandates of the national law (such as the state and its administrative agencies).[9]

Once *institutions* have been established and consolidated, human actions depend on what I will name *explicit* negotiations. These latter happen whenever the choices and attitudes of the individuals based in a certain *institution* comply

---

9   In this book, we focus on this second meaning (institutions as bodies mandated by the national law).

with a set of *institutional* rules acknowledged by various social actors. In this way, individual actions can be rapidly and easily understood by most members of society and as a result, the strength of the institution is enhanced. The conduct of a clinical trial, when it is acknowledged by a Research Foundation and ruled by a research contract, is very likely to depend on *explicit* negotiations. In other words, this activity is regulated by well-known, formal rules, which therefore are an expression of *explicit* processes.

In many countries that join global clinical trials, Research Foundations are becoming a widespread form, as more and more hospitals seem to be willing to manage payments and reimbursements in this way. However, the limits of standards and *explicit* negotiations create a range of voids for *implicit* arrangements and negotiations to appear. We start the analysis of this phenomenon in the following section and continue it in the next chapter.

2.4 Hybrid Work

As global trials constitute an ever-evolving activity, it is frequently difficult to subject all their aspects to the *explicit* institutional rules. Here, we can detect the dilemma described by Silveira (1996) as 'normative obsolescence': regulations are fixed forms that may rapidly fail to tame changing economic activities.

These challenges have become frequent in global trials, in which new schemes seem to emerge every day. One of the unforeseen effects of global trials in local sites has to do with workforce. In Spanish hospitals, for example, one finds two types of professionals. On the one hand, there is the 'traditional staff' providing health care services and whose work, *by law*, can only be paid with state resources. On the other hand, there are many research coordinators who deal with industrial trials and whose work is paid with resources collected from the trials industry by the Research Foundation. A co-investigator who is based in a hospital in Madrid told me that when a study requires procedures that are alien to the regular treatment of patients, the research team mobilizes and pays a nurse from the medical staff to undertake those procedures. Theoretically, the two hospital's sections should have few connections but in practice, then, there can be a constant flow of professionals crossing over those fluid borders.

Another interesting case was also observed in Madrid, where I visited another state hospital. Even though the Research Foundation has a physical space of its own, research coordinators do not work in the Foundation's offices, but are spread across the hospital. In many medical departments it is possible to bump into coordinators and their 'mini-offices', comprising computers, telephones, desks and their typical paper archives of clinical protocols and consent forms. I interviewed one of these coordinators, based in a haematology department. At the time of the interview, she had just been hired by the Research Foundation but, previously, she was working in the hospital with donations from companies, a sort of payment she calls 'scholarship' (*beca*):

> **In other specialties of the hospital, there are also people to do what you do.**
>
> *In some of them, but this is not that easy because, actually, our job is a bit complicated. As there is no one to pay us, because we are not involved by the Spanish public health, we need private funding. So if the departments are capable of getting this funding, then they are capable of hiring someone. But sometimes it is not that easy because ... Well, I've been here for six years and I spent four years with a scholarship, looking for sources so that people could pay me, donations from various pharmaceutical companies...*
>
> **And this scholarship was paid with resources...**
>
> *This scholarship is always paid with private money, with, say, donations from various pharmaceutical companies for certain projects. That is where the money comes from to pay the scholarship.*
>
> **Are there many people with similar scholarships?**
>
> *Yes ... Look, the situation is improving but, actually, at the beginning almost all the data managers of Spanish hospitals were like that, with scholarships...*

Global trials have promoted the emergence of new professionals and economic schemes in several hospitals across the world. Nowadays, when patients look for health care in a hospital, they may be moving in scenarios in which the borders between health care and research, as well as the distance between caregivers and the industry's acolytes, have become very fluid.

The blends promoted by global trials can involve physicians as well. In Pretoria, for example, doctors of both private and state hospitals are invited to fill in pre-screening forms sent by fax by a trials company. Through these forms, which are signed by the physician and the patient, the company can identify potential subjects for specific studies, subsequently phoning those people to propose participation. For sending back completed forms, as well as realizing successful indications of patients, physicians receive payments from the company. In this example, the working time itself denotes an *entanglement.* For in an appointment with a patient, the doctor is, *at the same time*, providing health care (an *explicit* role) and prospecting possible subjects for the trials company (an *implicit* function), being remunerated for both tasks.

It can be said that all patients are, at least potentially, joining the world of health and the world of trials *at the same time*. People looked after in hospitals may always be given more or less helpful medicines, referred to other institutions, assisted in their most pressing problems or proposed participation in a clinical trial. Nowadays, it is hard to find a key medical institution not running at least a small number of international studies. Therefore, caregivers are always fulfilling their medical tasks while prospecting potential research subjects. In this way, a hybrid work has been undertaken in hospitals and clinics all over the world. *Explicit* and *implicit* functions mingle, opening up much leeway for different types of agreements to be made.

2.5 The Dark Side of Research Contracts

In spite of the clarity brought about by the scheme depicted in Figure 2.1, in the everyday practice of trials many arrangements do escape the rules defined by institutions and contracts. For there are important questions that have not yet been addressed by national regulations. When it comes to the financial negotiations taking place within global trials, there is generally no difficulty pertaining to the reimbursements made to hospitals, especially when costs of medical procedures are substantially unified across the territory, as is the case in France. However, France and other countries have no guidelines for the medical staff's salary, a circumstance that can complicate the monetary assessments of the caregivers' work. In this way, payments to investigators are often a controversial issue, insofar as certain PIs may feel unhappy with the values offered by the trials industry and ask for higher amounts. The trials industry is very used to these negotiations and even anticipates them in big trials.

For CROs, dealing with individual investigators can sometimes prove more practical than talking to people based in medical administrative bodies, as we can see in the following quote from an interview with a Contract Specialist in Johannesburg:

For you, is it easier to deal with people [than with institutions]?

The private investigator, the doctor himself?

Yeah. Is it easier for you?

It is, it is in a way, because it is more ... You know, you find them, you can speak to them directly, you give them what they want, they ask for what they want, and there is no extra percentage that the institution will take or ... You know, the money he gets is the money he uses for the trial. If you deal with a government institution, they will want to keep 10 per cent of the budget for their own admin, their own overheads, and the difference goes to the doctor...

The universe of clinical trials is still laden with marks of abuses and unclear schemes that took place in the past. For example, as one physician-investigator interviewed in São Paulo recalls, payments to investigators used to be done in quite obscure ways:

For much time, all the institutions, and not only ours, you know, were doing research sponsored by the pharmaceutical industry behind the curtains, as you know. In the past it was like that, wasn't it? 'Oh, take this study, test some cases.' And they even paid the investigator in dollars.

And they paid directly to the investigator.

That is right. After that, all the regulations have come about, the good practices of clinical research and so on. And all the institutions had to rule that and create research committees and so on and all the ethics regulation has come about and so on. Things have improved a lot.

However, depending on the context, changes have not been very radical. In South Africa, for instance, the schemes of Figure 2.1 are simply lacking in a large number of cases. As we saw, the formal administration of South-African hospitals often has little participation, if any, in the negotiation and signature of research contracts. Even when the doctor is running the trial within a state hospital, contractual terms, including the study's budget and all the monetary flow, may be decided upon by the PI. him- or herself. In many cases, the investigator plays the role of Research Foundation, receiving all the resources and transferring them to people and services within the hospital. According to a Contract Specialist I interviewed in Johannesburg, the frequency of these schemes has been decreasing. If it is so, South Africa may be moving towards higher degrees of *institutionalization* in terms of monetary flows.

Here, it is important to point out two facts. First, when talking about South Africa, we are not dealing with a backward example. The country is a regional research hub, with high-skilled medical staff and modern sites, some of them having already been favourably assessed in audits of the FDA.[10] Second, as we shall see, clear rules and schemes can also fail in countries that might be considered the 'actual elite' of global trials.

Another deviation from the monetary pathways of Figure 2.1 has to do with the payment of taxes. In some hospitals (in France and some cases in Brazil), payments from companies can be received by investigators without being retained in an account within the Research Foundation. In those countries, investigators have elaborated schemes in order to receive payments without having to face income taxes, which would apply if they received resources in personal accounts.

In France, the solution was the creation of the so-called associations ('*associations*'), which emerged to receive and manage payments from different sources, including private companies. A physician interviewed in Paris argued that investigators are sometimes paralysed by the slow and bureaucratic procedures of hospitals; thus associations would enable them 'to solve in a fast way some material difficulties that may be faced by a [medical] department'. All those goals are indeed reachable through associations, but it seems that avoiding income tax is another major goal. Actually, associations are not an instrument to be used only in clinical research; there are indeed associations in several kinds of social domains, from arts to environmental causes. They were created, in French legislation, in 1900. Because they are non-profit organizations, their establishment does not imply the payment of taxes.

---

10 Food and Drug Administration, the American regulatory agency.

To be sure, associations can become a sort of Research Foundation and some of them have grown and become capable of ensuring the management of payments in less subjective ways.[11] However, it is known that many associations continue to be run as small bodies, sometimes involving the physicians of a department or even a single physician and a couple of employees. The point to be stressed here is that things become less and less clear-cut and sturdy as we go further into our analysis.

In Brazil, there is no such 'non-profit legal solution.' When the hospital has no Foundation, investigators often create private companies in order to receive payments from the trials industry. In Porto Alegre, I interviewed the Research Coordinator of a state hospital who spoke of this phenomenon. He explained that physicians cannot receive any money from the industry:

> How was this barrier circumvented? There are companies ... Researchers have constituted companies, legally, which sign tripartite contracts between the entity that is coordinating and distributing the resources in the country or abroad...
>
> **This entity is a CRO?**
>
> A CRO. So the CRO that is managing multicentre trials ... the investigator [with his or her company] and the hospital will sign a tripartite contract.
>
> **Okay. Okay. Excuse me, I think I haven't understood. The researcher has a company of him?**
>
> Of him ... Some of them have gathered to form a sole company and others have their own company, as they found it better.

With a company, the physician-entrepreneur, in addition to being able to receive private payments, can hire some staff to help conduct trials. Some of these companies may have up to 30 employees. However, these arrangements are becoming rare in Brazil, where most hospitals are adhering to the system illustrated in Figure 2.1.

---

11 The Association Claude Bernard and the Association Naturalia & Biologia are two examples of big associations in which large numbers of physicians gather.

However, even in countries and hospitals where *institutional* control is in place, a Research Foundation, an R&D Office or a Consortium cannot fully oversee parallel negotiations between the trials industry and investigators, due to the force of source agreements. Indeed, some physicians have found ways to circumvent the surveillance of Foundations, as explained by a CRO monitor in São Paulo:

> **Do you know if the costs to develop the study can vary importantly from hospital to hospital?**
>
> *Generally, the budget ... The payment is made per patient and the same amount for everybody. But, for example, there are institutions that ask for an overhead, as they call it, you know. So my institution allows me to use this room but I have to give them 20% of the payment made for each patient ... Then, the physician says [to the CRO]: 'Look, I cannot renounce to this 20%. I need you to pay me 20% more so that I can pay the institution and keep my 100% to run the study.' And this is negotiated with the sponsor. Some sponsors do agree and some sponsors do not.*

Of course, this extra payment that some physicians ask for cannot be made in front of the Foundations' eyes, because this would imply the retention of an 'extra-overhead'. We are dealing here with a hidden payment that escapes the institution's official control. Thus if on the one hand monetary flows are slowly being submitted to institutional mechanisms, on the other hand some actors are always identifying loopholes and 'tinkering with procedural standards,' to use Timmermans and Epstein's (2010, p. 81) expression in a different context.

As it was said, hospitals' services must be reimbursed for their participation in trials. In practice, this can only happen because whenever a patient is sent to a service, he or she will be identified as a research subject. However, in government institutions some physicians can simply neglect this information and refer people to a service without identifying them as research subjects. As a result, those people will undergo the medical procedures as normal patients of the hospital, and costs which might be met by the trial's sponsor, end up being surreptitiously transferred to the state. Arguably, this practice is adopted in many countries, as the result of source agreements. Thus the trials industry can save some money, probably providing part of these savings to physicians who adhere to the strategy.

Obviously, official information about all these arrangements is lacking. What seems sure is that some things continue to happen 'behind the curtains' of global trials. In an interview in Paris, a CRO's employee made the following declaration:

> *Often, when these sites ... when they make many, many patients, we ask the project team to send them a small thanking gift at the end of the study, or even during the study...*

> **And what is the gift?**

> *We don't have the right, we don't have the right to offer gifts any more. Before, there were many gifts that ... We don't have the right to do that any more [laughter.] Yes, it is forbidden. There was a time when they were invited to go to China ... But this is now forbidden...*

This interviewee, in a clear effort to behave kindly and friendly, forgot for a while that the situation consisted in an interview with a sociologist, and not a conversation with a colleague. The strong effort made to dispel the offer of gifts can only make wonder whether this practice has really come to an end. In the same way, the eagerness with which one French and one South-African physician told me, countless times during their interviews, that investigators 'don't earn anything' by running trials, suggests the hypothesis that even though they do not make money as clinical investigators, they may somehow benefit from playing the role of industry's scientific partners. When I talk about source agreements, I am referring precisely to these arrangements between the trials industry and some investigators, forming what could be thought of as the dark side of research contracts.

In this sense, source agreements would be comparable to the collusions between regulatory agencies and regulated industries, a phenomenon that has been named 'regulatory capture' (Huntington 1952; Stigler 1971; Kalt and Zupan 1990; Levine and Forrence 1990; Laffont and Tirole 1991). However, we are not dealing with collusions involving companies and state agencies, but with agreements between companies and certain professionals based in certain medical institutions, a type of negotiation that is even more difficult to detect and tame. For hospitals are further away from the steering force of state institutions than any regulatory agency responsible for taking care of national policies.

It is needless to say that for many physicians, clinical trials belong to a context in which health care and scientific knowledge are the main targets.[12] However, as a physician told me in Porto Alegre, the field of clinical trials is 'very heterogeneous; there are people making a living out of that'.

2.6 Global Trials and Local Agreements

As we have seen, negotiations can be carried out in *explicit* ways, but they can also follow *implicit* patterns. *Implicit* negotiations come into play whenever individuals who are based in a certain *institution* find loopholes or voids in order to make choices and install activities whose occurrence escape the full control of the institution and which are, therefore, hard to interpret for the majority of social actors. In a clinical trial, payments made outside of the overseeing scope of the medical institution would happen as *implicit* attitudes. Therefore, actions undertaken in clinical research have crucial political and social impacts. Depending on the processes adopted to make choices, the final result can lead to either *democratic* or *conspiratorial* arrangements.

In addition to studying the nature of social actions, it is important to understand the ways in which they are connected to (or disconnected from) the institutional life of a country. *Democratic* schemes cannot emerge without social arrangements reinforcing the set of national *institutions*. In the *theory of communicative action*, the ideas of *institution*, law and state are more important than one might suppose at first sight. If the *communication* that crosses over a social group is not solidified and objectified through the production of law and effective institutions, final social arrangements would suffer from a severe lack of legitimacy. 'The procedure of lawmaking must ... be legally institutionalized if it is to guarantee the equal inclusion of all members of the political community in the democratic process of opinion- and will-formation' (Habermas 2008, p. 79).

In spite of the proliferation of global standards and local rules, there is still much leeway for *validity* in clinical research, creating voids that may be filled by *implicit* arrangements, in a domain that is frequently organized by unspecific regulations. In addition, global companies have quick and easy access to physician-investigators, a circumstance that invites them to make individual (rather than institutional) agreements. In many countries, CROs can easily buy databases of physicians, contact and invite them to join global clinical studies.

---

12   On this topic, see Chapter 3.

Some physicians may feel at ease when receiving proposals from, and negotiating with, multinational companies. However, this can be misleading, because pharma companies are heavily equipped to engage in profitable negotiations and can be fiercely defended whenever they hire CROs. In Johannesburg, a Contract Specialist described the way in which a CRO would prevent sponsors from being deceived by local financial matters:

> *But can the sponsor tell you: 'Oh, for this trial the doctors must receive this amount'?*
>
> *... They do tell us but then I'll tell them they [the doctors] don't need that much. I'll push back to the sponsor and say: 'You know, he should only receive 2,000 Rand, I'm not going to give him 20 [thousand rand]' ... So I'll say to the sponsor: 'Look, that is too much money, in South Africa we don't pay so much money, we only pay 1,000 rand' ... Obviously, it is to their benefit, you know. If they don't have to pay 1,000 rand and they only have to pay 100, they'll keep the difference.*

Thus we would be wrong to conclude that only rigid standards (*facticity*) prevail in global trials. Indeed, there is much space for negotiations and uncertainties (*validity*). However, the most decisive negotiations tend to take place as *implicit* phenomena, away from the steering force of *institutions*. As Petryna (2009, p. 187) claimed: 'A largely uncharted field of global experimental activity has been taking form over the past decades – sometimes beyond what established regulations can control or even keep track of.'

Slowly, we get away from open discussions and from what Habermas (1996) called 'parliamentary complex', that is, the universe of institutions and democratic debate. As a result, *conspiratorial* schemes (as opposed to *democratic* ones) are emerging everywhere, increasing the weight of *implicit* processes and roles. However, the very same domain of global trials can also be explored by local actors in order to fulfil their *explicit* functions in creative ways. To understand this phenomenon, we highlight the exploration of the medical potentialities of trials in the following chapter.

3

Care: The Global Need for Global Trials

In the previous chapters, some of the *instrumental* aspects of trials were highlighted. However, every trial entails the recruitment of patients, the establishment of personal relationships, and the activation of local traditions, in a word, a whole set of *communicational* aspects. Therefore, we must learn to look at global trials in the light of two different and complementary *rationalities*. As for the manifestation of the *communicational rationality* in clinical research, it is hard to really grasp it without paying attention to the 'microprocesses that take place in a given [research] setting' (Mueller 1997, p. 58). In Will and Moreira's (2010, p. 13) words, we need to focus on 'those contextual factors that shape what a trial can do'.

The economic flows of clinical trials, for instance, can be seen either as expressions of payments and profits (their instrumental side, previously explored in this book) or expressions of income (their communicational side). In order to make this distinction clear, this chapter focuses on the hidden provision of income within clinical trials.

Some social science studies explored the issue of payments and reimbursements made to research subjects within a clinical trial. Looking forfor quick money, some people may try to enrol in clinical studies, sometimes participating in several successive trials and becoming a sort of professional subject (Fisher 2009; Abadie 2010). For those people, joining a clinical trial is the result of a practical, almost technical calculation, as Fisher points out: 'Serial patient-subjects I interviewed described how the amount of money associated with completing a study enters into their decision making about whether they want to enrol' (2009, p. 139).

These practices are becoming common in the United States, where the economic aspects of trials can be largely explored by ordinary citizens. The same phenomenon does occur, albeit less frequently, in countries whose sites conduct phase 1 trials[1] (such as the UK, Spain and France), where participants are reimbursed for the inconveniences caused by the study's procedures. For instance, as students tend to form a less affluent population eagerly seeking money to pay the bills, phase 1 trials can turn into an attractive option to them.

In South Africa, the national regulatory agency determined a minimum amount to be reimbursed to subjects in each visit to a research site.[2] If the person travels a relatively short distance by using either the state or popular means of transport, this amount can certainly surpass (perhaps by far) the actual costs incurred by the participant, including transport (both ways) and one meal. In all countries, the amounts of reimbursements or payments are clearly stated in the 'informed consent' forms, and as Fisher (2009) noted in the case of the United States, this is sometimes the only information that subjects consider before consenting to participation.

In spite of the relevance of these phenomena, it is important to note that they are considerably restrained by ethical and regulatory concerns. In all of the five countries involved in my study, ethics committees would immediately oppose a phase 2, 3 or 4 trial in which subjects receive payments. Sometimes, committees are even reluctant to allow simple reimbursements for transport expenses and other costs entailed by participation.

Nevertheless, ethics committees, administrators, policy-makers and analysts have been unable to identify a surreptitious economic flow taking place in global trials. As I will claim, these studies imply the gathering of crucial economic resources (in the form of clinical data), which is compensated by the provision of health care. These hidden exchanges deserve to be unveiled and analysed, for even though they do not assume a *monetary* form, they constitute a new and important form of *economic* relationship. We shall focus on seven topics: the formation of a 'medical elite' in global trials; the therapeutic dimensions of clinical research; medical decisions taken in trials; the issue of protocols' inclusion and exclusion criteria; clinical negotiations between physicians and companies; the conceptual difference between *health care* and

---

1   Roughly speaking the development of a drug, from the isolation of a molecule to the final approval of the medicine, is divided into four clinical phases. In each phase, a larger population of subjects is recruited.
2   The minimum amount established by the Medicines Control Council is 150 South-African rand.

therapy; and the expansion of 'disposable income' through the provision of health care within clinical studies.

3.1 Who are Key Opinion Leaders?

It is hard to determine the exact proportion of physicians who engage in clinical research, a figure that most hospitals lack. However, there are two phenomena that appear to be certain. First, the majority of physicians do not participate in industrial research. Second, hospitals linked to universities hold a bigger proportion of physician-investigators, but it is difficult to say whether many of them take part in studies sponsored by the trials industry or not. In a private (non-academic) hospital in Porto Alegre, there are 20 physicians based in the department of oncology; 6 doctors take part in industrials trials whereas 14 have never done so.

Due to historical and social features, the rarity of clinical researchers can be even greater in some countries. In South Africa, for instance, the long period of apartheid kept clinical research as the privilege of a few (white) doctors who managed to gain experience and expertise. In Johannesburg, I interviewed the Managing Director of a local CRO, who told me:

> **When we think about your sites in South Africa and your investigators here, is it possible to compare your database and the database of the biggest CROs?**
>
> *You would be able to, because the thing is that South Africa is not a huge pool of doctors [engaged in industrial trials]. So, for example, if you look at oncology, everybody, pharma companies, big CROs and us would all go to the same seven or eight oncologists for a trial. If you're looking at your general practitioner, where you're doing a pneumonia study or an antibiotic study, then your pool is wider but, again, we all tend to go back to people we've worked with before and you know you're going to get the patients, the quality data...*

In order to counter this tendency, the South-African government, through its regulatory agency for drugs and trials (the Medicines Control Council), is advancing a policy called capacity-building element. Companies conducting trials in the country are invited to include new sites and investigators into their studies so that research expertise can be dispersed across the territory.

If companies wish to work with only 'traditional' sites and investigators, the choice must be carefully justified. To get regulatory approval, companies are not obliged to meet this requirement, but 'it is becoming harder and harder to get approval without that' according to a Director of Clinical Management of a multinational CRO.

Among many other things, CROs are responsible for identifying the most skilled physicians for a certain study. There is a type of physician who very often takes part in global trials: the so-called 'key opinion leaders.' In the UK, a Vice-President for Clinical Management defined these professionals:

> *They probably perceive themselves to be at the top of the pile. In reality they are, because they all are experts in that therapy area, they know more about the disease than probably anybody else in the world .... Yes, I guess they are the elite of trialists.*

Opinion leaders frequently associate their activities as caregivers with the role of professors and scientists. Frequently, they have long-lasting relations to pharma companies (for example, they can be hired as scientific advisors) and in some instances they may participate in the initial design of the industrial study's protocol. Their presence creates a hierarchy within the universe of trials, for as the same interviewee described:

> *There are the very influential doctors who know about science and are very big in the therapy field, and these are the people who help design the protocols ... The others are people, generally, who just are good at doing trials, you know, they have good populations, the right sources of patients, they understand the requirements of trials, they have the research staff that are dedicated to run the studies. So that is the other group, I would say, they are more the people you go to to get the study run.*[3]

Opinion leaders are very frequently based in key health and research institutions, a circumstance that reinforces their leading position. As Fisher (2009) noted before, they are very busy professionals and consequently, seldom good recruiters, that is, their participation in the study does not entail the inclusion of many research subjects. However, pharmaceutical companies strive

---

3 Actually, the trials industry treasures both opinion leaders and good recruiters. If they leave the hospital in which they are based, the industry will certainly strive to keep the relationship in their new location.

to rely on the participation of these eminent professionals, in order to impart more scientific legitimacy to studies and products. If the trials enterprise is meant to generate evidence on the scientific quality of a drug, then the presence of opinion leaders in a study is one of appropriate ways to reach this target.

As we shall see,[4] this hierarchy of investigators is quite useful for the trials industry. Being capable of dealing with a small group of eminent researchers increases the control that companies have over the whole enterprise. The majority of investigators lack the prestige and scientific authority to engage in hard negotiations with huge corporations. In spite of the political power of multinational companies, some physicians, and especially opinion leaders, try to explore the medical potentialities of global trials by approaching pharma companies to propose research projects, as we see in the next sections.

3.2 What is a Therapeutic Trial?

During my fieldwork I tried to verify whether, from the physicians' viewpoint, a clinical trial can only be considered as scientific research or also a therapeutic alternative. Some physicians hastened to convey the pure scientific nature of trials, as done by a cardiologist interviewed in Porto Alegre:

> *[...] in your opinion, a clinical trial must be considered as research or a therapeutic alternative?*
>
> *As research. As research, otherwise it would not be a clinical trial; it would be an established therapy. If the truth about that form of treatment was already known, it would no longer be necessary to run a clinical trial.*

However, it is interesting to note that the majority of principal investigators to whom this question was asked acknowledge that clinical trials can have purposes going beyond the advancement of scientific knowledge of diseases and drugs. Some of them were rather cautious, such as a paediatrician based in Paris:

> *Do investigators, physicians, consider clinical trials as research or therapy?*
>
> *As research ... It may sometimes be therapy but it is mainly research.*

---

4   Sections 3.5 to 3.8.

Sometimes therapy ... In which cases?

For example, in rare diseases. We have a lot of rare diseases here in the hospital, orphan diseases, and in this case it is an actual therapy. It is no longer exclusively research, it is mainly therapy for the child, in order to try to save the child.

Some physicians admitted a blend of purposes, as a cardiologist based in São Paulo did:

From the point of view of physicians, is a clinical study therapy or research?

Both things. Both things. In a clinical study, when a medicine is used, you are in fact testing a new therapy or a new way to apply that product for the patient's treatment. So the physician provides it as health care and research. Things are intertwined. Actually, both sides are present all the time.

Finally, some of them directly stressed the therapeutic dimension of trials, as an oncologist based in Madrid did:

Do physicians see clinical trials as pure investigation or also as a therapeutic alternative?

I believe we see it mainly as treatment. It is a treatment that serves to advance knowledge, but it is a treatment that tries to improve what has already been commercialized, what is conventional. So we consider it as a possibility to improve what is already available.

Vallejo developed a typology of clinical investigators, identifying four groups: 1. 'Up and comers' are prospecting the domain of trials and looking for career options within medicine; 2. 'Business-driven' doctors are seeking for economic advantages; 3. 'Compound developers' are striving to raise medical discoveries and heighten the level of scientific knowledge; and 4. 'Healers' are precisely those who are concerned with the treatment offered to patients within a trial (Vallejo 2006, pp. 189–190).

Thus for some physicians, clinical studies are considered to have therapeutic goals above all. This perspective is understandable, as in some trials, and especially those of phase 4, research subjects undergo already approved health care procedures and while treatment is provided, there is collection of data in order to further gauge the therapy's effects. Therefore, in clinical trials there is a blend of research and care, as firstly noted by Renée Fox (1998, p. 53), in whose words clinical researchers must face a difficult 'conflict between their obligations to advance knowledge and their responsibility to promote the welfare of their patient-subjects'. Fox focused on a medical ward in which clinical research was in its early stages, making experiments quite 'perilous'. Nowadays, with the assimilation of trials into the *reality* of hospitals and the emergence of modern technologies and procedures, this coexistence between the advancement of 'knowledge', on the one hand, and concerns with the patients' 'welfare', on the other, has lost some its characteristics of conflict to acquire traits of partnership.

Moreover, the terminology of trials itself underpins the therapeutic approach of some physicians. For instance, there is a type of study called 'therapeutic trial' in which investigators firmly expect the drug to benefit research subjects. A therapeutic trial would be, for example, a phase 3 study on a drug that showed very favourable effects in all previous phases, provoking, among physicians and sponsors, strong confidence pertaining to its efficacy and safety. An even stronger example would be a phase 4 trial involving a medicine that has already been approved and launched into the market. In this case, even though a study is conducted, the compound has already been assimilated into the available pool of official medications, enhancing significantly the investigators' confidence.

Due to the recognition of these therapeutic capacities, clinical trials tend to become a normal part of medical calculations made by physicians. In order to unravel this phenomenon, we shall focus, in the following section, on the ways in which physicians assess clinical protocols and incorporate trials into the *reality* of hospitals.

3.3 Clinical Trials and Medical Decisions

As soon as caregivers acknowledge certain therapeutic aspects in trials, these are taken into account whenever medical choices are made. When dealing with the problems presented by their patients, physicians have, on the one hand, the knowledge assimilated throughout their years of study and, on the other hand, a set of medicines and therapies approved by their peers and national agencies.

At the same time, the conduct of trials is also underpinned by the standards of medicine and approved by official regulatory agencies. In this way, trials may end up being considered as one of the alternatives available to deal with diseases and medical problems. This is the view of a cardiologist working in Porto Alegre:

> **From the point of view of physicians, is a clinical trial considered as research or a therapeutic alternative?**
>
> *[Pause.] It depends, I think. There is no answer for that ... It depends on the case. Some time ago we put a patient into a study and for him it was a therapeutic alternative but it can be research. It is both things, I think.*

In particularly pressing contexts, clinical trials may be regarded as a very reasonable medical option. In Johannesburg, a principal investigator told me:

> *Generally, there are indigent and poor patients in this hospital, right, who can't afford state-of-the-art, highly expensive, you know, new medications. So if we put half a dozen of the patients onto a clinical trial, we've got access to a state-of-the-art drug...*

The moral worth of such stances toward clinical trials is an issue that I reserve for bioethicists. To employ a word of historical weight to sociologists, I am focusing on the *praxis* of physicians, that is, the ways in which they act in particular circumstances, being informed by personal preferences but also by the configuration of their social milieu. What is important to stress here is that even though clinical protocols are designed by pharma companies or CROs, doctors are not passive followers of rules.

> *In observing the utilization of procedural guidelines in medical practices, it is striking that patients and medical personnel are not turned into mindless followers of some preset recipe. From their perspectives, the guideline is drawn upon to advance their own goals and professional trajectories. For all those involved, the guideline is not a goal in itself but a means, acted upon in terms of their own aims and the local constraints structuring the situation in which the guideline happens to be placed (Timmermans and Berg 2003, p. 70).*

What is more, clinical studies, instead of instilling a passive attitude amongst physicians, ask for surveillance and multiply the number of medical choices to be made. Three phenomena can be noted.

First, physicians frequently assess the scientific worth of trials. This cautiousness is particularly important for those who are suspicious about the trials industry, considering that companies may advance low-quality studies in order to grasp business opportunities. According to a cardiologist interviewed in Paris:

> *In clinical research, as in everywhere else, there is good clinical research, average clinical research and mediocre clinical research ... So clinical research is not immune to imperfections and inaccuracies. So there are trials that are more or less interesting, more or less important.*

Therefore, as Mueller (2004, p. 47) noted before, physicians are frequently willing to gauge 'the scientific merits of the trial' even though, as this same French physician put it, 'this is often something that has a relatively subjective nature. It is not as objective as we would desire. People can turn out to have divergent opinions about current standards of medicine and science...'

To be sure, the physicians' scientific evaluations can be distorted by economic purposes they may pursue, as previously illustrated in this book. However, some impartial assessments do occur, and some institutions have even developed mechanisms to make choices less dependent on individual stances. In London, for instance, I visited a clinical trial unit of a university hospital where there is a scientific advisory board responsible for reviewing protocols to be developed there. This board is composed of more than 20 members, including physicians, nurses, scientists and lay members. Another example is the clinical research unit of a state hospital in Paris, where all studies must be approved by a scientific committee that would reject, for instance, a trial whose principal investigator is conducting too many studies at the same time. In these examples, high degrees of *institutionalization* led to more disciplined attitudes and made *conspiratorial* arrangements less likely to occur.

Second, some physicians or research teams may elaborate their list of priorities, being more willing to accept new studies on certain disease areas than others. A Research Coordinator who works for a group of hospitals in London told me:

Take cancer for example ... There is a team of nurses and coordinators and managers that work in each site, that support cancer studies ... So what will happen is that they will say: 'Here is another study for this PI.' And they will say: 'No. We can't have any more studies because we don't need any more breast studies, we want colorectal. So we're not taking any more breast studies.'

Who says that?

The cancer team, the team ... They meet and they discuss the studies and they talk about new ones, they have a board meeting on whether they will take those new ones...

In this case, therefore, individual decisions are given up for the benefit of collective assessments.

Finally, when looking for physicians to conduct some studies, the trials industry has to be prepared for negative answers. Sometimes, physicians refuse participation in a trial, considering the compound to be tested as unnecessary or unpromising. Some physicians, or even whole hospitals, may be more academic-centred, and therefore less willing to participate in most industrial studies. For example, a physician based in a hospital in Paris told me:

So economically, it is more interesting ... to work with pharmaceutical companies than with institutional studies.

Yes and no. Yes, because we are going to ask more from the industry in terms of service and costs but, on the other hand, sometimes the type of study we're going to do with the pharmaceutical industry is not as interesting as purely institutional studies ... And we manage to do very, very good studies, which are published in big journals, whereas the pharmaceutical industry will propose us trials they are interested in (assessing their medicines, comparing them to a reference) but that for us, scientifically, is of little interest ... If we are to choose between an institutional study and an industrial study, we will tend to choose the institutional study.

Investigators, then, develop their criteria to assess the relevance of trials. For a Spanish rheumatologist, for instance, the use of placebos would be a reason for denying participation: 'Having a patient with a serious disease for thirty or forty weeks on a trial doesn't seem correct to us [in the ward]; it doesn't seem ethical to us, while we have medicines to control that disease.' A French cardiologist gave me another example:

> *I remember a clinical trial in which we were asked to withhold antiplatelet therapy[5] until randomization, whereas our practice is to give antiplatelet treatment as soon as possible. We refused to participate in that trial...*

In addition, some loopholes of clinical research can be utilized by physicians in order to develop therapeutic tactics. For instance, some people consider the conduct of competing trials (that is, simultaneous studies on different drugs to treat the same disease) as an unethical practice. This, critics say, amounts to 'medical gambling', because the physician would be relaxing medical surveillance and submitting patients to the hazards of experimentation. However, some doctors accumulate competing trials in order to compare outcomes and gain knowledge of the therapeutic efficacy of different compounds under study. A CRO's monitor based in Madrid told me that some physicians voice their disappointment toward a molecule being tested in a trial: 'Sometimes, the physician says: "Look, your product is worse for my patients than that of another company which is also running a clinical trial." There are parallel competing trials, running in the same site, with the same investigator.'

Arguably, from the point of view of many physicians, every clinical trial is initially regarded as a therapeutic trial, or at least a potentially therapeutic trial. In other words, global trials can be framed as sources of *instruments* (that is, useful objects with which local needs are better fulfilled) with which concrete health problems can be solved or minimized. Thus *mediational actors* have learnt that, in their relation to *instrumental actors*, some *instruments* can be selected and used to reach immediate goals. Therefore, the *mediational action* activates, in local contexts, *instruments* that would otherwise be always out of the patients' reach. From a sociological standpoint, clinical protocols, cutting-edge medicines, therapeutic trials, in a nutshell *instruments* are the most precious discovery that local actors have ever managed to realize.

The medical decisions taken by physicians when dealing with clinical studies are made through *explicit* assessments. If asked, those physicians would explain and *justify* their behaviour based on institutional rules and medical traditions that are largely recognized. Certainly, some factors (like economic

---

5   A therapy that inhibits thrombosis.

ones) may direct the caregivers' choices away from medical criteria. However, on many occasions they do not abdicate their therapeutic responsibilities and therefore frame global trials as an *instrument* with which their *explicit* medical functions can be better fulfilled. In other, more personal words, 'we'd never do a trial that we feel is not beneficial to the patient,' as a Research Pharmacist put it in Johannesburg. In even more direct words, 'I wouldn't participate in trials which I think are rubbish' according to a P.I. based in London.

Nevertheless, the previous chapters contain some evidence that medical purposes are unlikely to always prevail in global trials. In certain situations, one can even speak of a clash between therapeutic needs and business interests or, more precisely, between the *communicational* and the *instrumental rationalities*. In the middle of these opposing trends, the *mediational action* needs to provide answers and survive. The following section aims to unravel these paradoxes.

3.4 Criteria to Include or Exclude People

In every clinical protocol, it is necessary to determine the criteria according to which people may or may not be selected for the study. In the hierarchy of protocols, inclusion criteria are always overruled by exclusion criteria. For instance, even if a patient has a certain disease that is an inclusion criterion, this person will not be recruited if he or she smokes and smoking is an exclusion criterion.

In São Paulo, I interviewed a Research Coordinator based in a private oncologic practice offering health care to a very wealthy surrounding population. As oncologic treatments can have sky-rocketing prices, even these affluent patients can find it difficult to afford some medicines. Clearly, access can be harder for poor populations. In the same city, in an interview with an oncologist based in a hospital, this issue was addressed once more:

> *I imagine that as your patients are of a lower socio-economic level, it is sometimes very important for them to be included in a certain study, so that they can have access to a certain therapy ...*

> *To a new drug ... If you have a new drug available, you know, and you believe that it will be beneficial for the patient, it would be the ideal situation to put as many patients as possible [into the study]. But the inclusion criteria of clinical protocols are very rigid, you know. So you*

don't manage to put as many patients as you would like to ... Firstly, because of the patients' selection. I cannot make the patient fit all the criteria to be included. Another difficulty is the number of cases ... If I've agreed to include 20 patients, you know, I cannot include 40 ... That is established beforehand.

Thus the therapeutic concerns held by physician-investigators can be frustrated by the standards of a global trial. On the one hand, physicians may be favourable to the inclusion of big numbers of patients. On the other, as exclusion criteria are the strongest rule in the game of trials, the whole enterprise has acquired a bias toward the exclusion of people. This trend is reinforced by the proliferation of medicines exploring niche markets, requiring stricter and stricter criteria. Eventually, the trials industry is shooting at very peculiar clinical targets and looking for 'the right patients for the drug' as Lakoff (2007) stressed in his study on trials for antidepressant drugs.

To do so, they have come up with strategies to both satisfy the regulatory demand to test their medications on coherent populations of 'depressed' subjects, and, at the same time, to hone their subject group to include only those who are most likely to respond to medication (Lakoff 2007, p. 70).

From the trials industry's vantage point, the globalization of clinical research expands the likeliness of finding research subjects to recruit. However, from the point of view of potential subjects, the design of very strict inclusion and exclusion criteria turns participation into a rare event. What is more, the exclusion of people from a clinical trial continues to be decided upon by individual corporations, as well as investigators who may maintain close relations to them. Rather than happening in the open 'parliamentary complex' (Habermas 1996), those negotiations take place in *conspiratorial* arenas where established *institutions* do not have a say. This issue, as well as the twofold nature of global trials, is analysed in the following section.

3.5 Clinical Agreements

In the previous chapters, it was shown that source agreements can modify the monetary flows of clinical trials. Companies and investigators can also negotiate on the conditions in which research subjects will be treated within a trial. In some circumstances, physicians can use these opportunities to glean some therapeutic results.

An interesting example was verified in London, in a clinic for smoking-related diseases. One of the investigators of this clinic, an eminent professor who is also based in a key English university, proposed, to a top multinational company, a study on a medicine produced by the firm. The psychologist of this research team summarizes the process:

> *we approached the pharmaceutical company to say we wanted to do an academic study and whether they would sponsor that. So it is on a very modest budget. It is not, you know, millions-of-pounds kind of project. It is something we've developed and they said they would like to sponsor. It is called an investigator-initiated project.*

As a result of this source agreement, the company sponsored the study, being responsible for meeting all costs involved. The medicine was provided for free for a couple of months, during the duration of the trial. In January 2011, in addition to this study, the clinic was running two investigator-initiated projects. In this therapeutic domain trials are quite big, involving from 100 to 200 research subjects. The large size of the sample is offset by the short period of the study, which lasts only a few months. During this time, and thanks to agreements between companies and investigators, participants have free access to a registered medicine. In this way, some patients may end up gleaning some advantages from the initiatives taken by physician-investigators. If this example does not sound very telling, let's look at other, more impressive stories.

In Johannesburg, a rheumatologist told me that in some studies, investigators can ask the pharma company to continue to provide the medicine on completion of a trial, if it is found to be beneficial. In this way, the compound would continue to be accessed by the research subjects for a reduced price, if not for free:

> *So it is almost like, you know, we are committed to four or five state [hospital's] patients. Can we get the medication which is very useful at half the price for the state patients? Or can they give a certain amount of drug on a compassionate basis, free, you know, for the patients? So I think it is almost like an advocacy group for the patient to get access to those medications…*

By 'advocating' for patients, investigators would therefore be able to ensure the access to a medicine by means of agreements with the trials industry.

The analysis of the Brazilian situation is also helpful to grasp the presence of *validity*, as well as medical sagacity, in clinical research. Most Brazilian hospitals still operate in the precarious conditions generated by long-lasting State negligence. Some Brazilian physicians, or at least those who are capable of negotiating with multinational companies, may try to compensate this dearth of medical resources through the establishment of agreements with corporations.

One example was given by a Research Coordinator working in a cardiologic centre in São Paulo. As she patiently explained to me, clinical studies are often conceived by the PIs of the hospital, who approach pharma companies to propose clinical studies. Thanks to this kind of agreement, some physicians of this hospital have been able to access a medical device that is called pharmacological stent. A stent is a small tube that is permanently implanted into a patient's artery to normalize the blood flux. The technique firstly appeared in the mid-1990s and about ten years ago a new generation of stents was created, bringing about an upheaval in the field of angioplasty. The so-called pharmacological stent is a device that contains a drug. Previous clinical studies are said to have shown bigger benefits for patients who receive pharmacological stents, as the device reduces the occurrence of adverse events as well as mortality rates.

The interviewee works in the department of angioplasty of the hospital, which means that all clinical trials conducted there involve the implantation of stents, be it in the normal or pharmacological version. She explains that pharmacological stents, due to their high costs, are not yet provided by the state. However, by conducting a clinical trial it is possible to access this technology, a circumstance that ensures very quick recruitment of many patients. In her words, 'the recruitment is amazingly quick because we are providing something that is really used in private hospitals within a hospital that lacks it'.

Contrarily to what one might expect, the hospital has to buy the stent to be used in these trials. Health care and research are completely *entangled* in this case. Patients receive a device which is already approved either in Brazil or other countries. Thus the intervention is done as a normal health care procedure. At the same time, the research subject (which means the patient) will provide some data about his or her health condition after the operation, and the information is used to enhance the knowledge of the stent. On the one hand, as the device is part of health care provided to the patient, the industry can argue that it must be (as it really is) bought as normal therapy. On the other hand, investigators can also bargain by claiming that the research efforts of the hospital and its patients must be compensated somehow. As national and international standards of clinical research are deaf and silent in the face of such impasses, there is some leeway for an *implicit* agreement to emerge. According to this Research Coordinator:

> *In most cases the stent is bought, in phase 4 studies. It is not all the cases. But these agreements happen between the sponsor and the investigator. I cannot tell you the details.*

> **But do you know where the resources for buying the stent come from?**

> *Well, when they establish an agreement, it is the same price the state would pay for a normal stent. So it buys a superior stent, which is the pharmacological one, at the same price. They establish this agreement … It is like the hospital would spend x to buy a non-pharmacological stent for the patient. Then we have a study … Then they establish an agreement. 'Look, the sponsor will ask for the same price and provide a stent which is used in private hospitals where the price is 3x, but they agree about a lower price to run the study…*

By using the force they have as key opinion leaders, these physicians end up providing, within a state hospital, a cutting-edge technology only available in private hospitals, without pushing the state toward further expenses. From the patients' point of view, the arrangement is also interesting because having access to such an expensive technology amounts to a serendipitous event.

This is the force of source agreements, which have a clear social impact. For they may enable the provision of health care[6] within a clinical trial that, from the viewpoint of research subjects and investigators, turns into treatment. Thus I can only agree with Petryna (2009, p. 30) when she argues that 'the line between what counts as experimentation and what counts as medical care is in flux'.

---

6   Here I am really speaking of *health care* and not about *therapy*. On this difference, see section 3.6.

At the same time, the frontier between the *instrumental* and *communicational rationalities* also gets blurred. On the one hand, this sort of agreement makes it possible for physicians to solve medical problems and access expensive medicines or devices. On the other hand, however, such agreements happen in the closed relationship between the trials industry and physician-investigators. Many sites are state-owned hospitals but by engaging in these negotiations, physicians end up reinforcing the operations of multinational companies and undermining the steering role that their institutions might play. To be sure, regulatory agencies and ethics committees review the process and can refuse the conduct of a protocol. However, these reviewing tasks are frequently carried out by an overburdened staff that may be lacking the appropriate expertise to delve into the methodological complexities (as well as some scientific traps) of clinical protocols (Bicudo 2012).

From a medical point of view, source agreements may favour the solution of immediate health troubles, helping physicians to fulfil their *explicit* functions as caregivers. From a political standpoint, however, crucial problems can derive from these hidden agreements (these *conspiracies*) promoted by companies and some investigators. Even though they are aware of their choices, the dialogue they undertake is necessarily and exclusively laden with technical and medical concerns. The trials industry and investigators may develop the whole process without considering that their decisions will affect populations, the economic dynamics of countries, or the weight of world regions within the global geography of trials. By considering medical procedures, economic targets, clinical strategies and other similarly technical issues, companies and researchers are in a sense formulating *implicit* scientific and health policies that escape most forms of *institutional* control.

In this way, the medical potentialities of trials, which were highlighted previously, are limited. In addition, one might argue, it is risky to speak of actual medical autonomy in the domain of industrial studies. Indeed, the trials industry has learnt to use many statistical tools that may enhance the likeness of getting favourable results (Sackett et al. 2003; Busfield 2006; Petryna 2009) or salvage a trial that has led to unfavourable outcomes (Abraham 1993; Sackett et al. 2003; Turner et al. 2008; McGoey and Jackson 2009). Thus it might be asked whether physicians are being deceived by the trials industry, which would be simply embellishing poor clinical protocols, elaborating misleading scientific methodologies, and luring doctors into appealing, albeit worthless, studies. Global trials would then amount to huge placebos given to well-intentioned physicians.

Although this objection is very important, it can take us away from the sociological interpretation I am proposing here. If we were to provide a medical response, it would be necessary to cross a complicated labyrinth of examinations, biological concepts, scientific arguments ... and clinical trials. Fortunately, it is possible to continue to follow our sociological pathway by considering that even though clinical research can have poor or absent medical effects, therefore lacking *therapy*, there is always a component of *health care* in clinical trials. Here, it is important to make this conceptual distinction clear.

3.6 Therapy and Care

As Kohlen (2009, p. 108) wisely stressed, one has to avoid drawing a drastic separation between 'patient-oriented care' and 'illness-oriented cure', for an extreme division would lead to 'a simplified understanding of medicine'. Bearing this warning in mind, I will nevertheless proceed to distinguish between *therapy* and *care* because disentangling these two elements of medical practice can help to build up a socio-economic interpretation of clinical trials. This effort has not to do with theoretical dilettantism; it is rather aimed to reproduce, at the empirical level of trials, the conceptual division between the *instrumental* and *communicational* rationalities, which is crucial in the theory of communicative action (Habermas 1987, 1996).

In talking about *therapy*, I refer to every kind of medical intervention (an operation, provision of medicine, psychological procedure, among others) whose outcome is the solution or alleviation of a medicalized problem. This outcome can be verified via tests and assessments that are also typical to modern medicine (scans, laboratory tests, imaging examinations, among others). We can assume, for example, the situation of a cancer patient whose disease would demonstrate a certain regression after the application of some medical procedure. Of course, this definition is quite problematic, for it is sometimes difficult to conclude that improvement and alleviation have really been obtained, but such details and complications are not decisive in a sociological explanation in which a high level of medical accuracy is not necessary.

Therapy has to do with outcomes and is informed by general concepts about disease; in its turn, *health care* is rather a process and, more precisely, a social process involving interpersonal relations in particular contexts. There is *care* whenever one person dedicates some time and attention to some other person who is considered to be sick, therefore deserving special treatment. Thus my definition is quite similar to that provided by Gilligan (1982) and Noddings (1984) when they framed care (or *caring*) as a set of actions and decisions adopted in concrete contexts. My distinction between *therapy* and *care* also reflects, in a certain sense, the distinction between 'care' and 'cure' proposed by Gadow (1985).

These two dimensions are always present in medical acts. However, it is important to conceptually disentangle them in order to organize an interpretative scheme. In addition, the distinction is helpful because, influenced by Foucault's (1988, 1999) ideas, some social scientists tend to foreground the relevance of *therapy* (with its elements of social control) and disregard the role played by *care* (with its communitarian aspects). Hence the importance of some ideas proposed by thinkers who placed care and morality at the core of medicine (Benner 1989; Tronto 1993).

Moreover care, as an interpersonal phenomenon par excellence, is a fruitful concept for sociological interpretation, offsetting the weight of biomedical and technical approaches to medicine. As Kohlen (2009, pp. 126–127) claimed in her review of Benner's theory: 'a technological and decontextualized understanding of health and illness leaves caring practices and social goods obscured and undermined'. Thus even though the distinction I am making does not have far-reaching implications, it does allow us to construct a socio-economic interpretation of clinical research.

It is widely recognized that global trials, because of the presence of multinational companies, are laden with economic concerns. Perhaps this very notion is what makes it difficult to see that at the local level and in concrete research sites, global trials spawn relations and phenomena barely anticipated and controlled by the trials industry. To be sure, raising evidence about a pharmaceutical compound's efficacy and safety, one of the major goals of trials, is directly informed by the search for profits and economic success that is typical of capitalistic companies. Nevertheless, these targets cannot be pursued without the conduct of clinical procedures entailing more or less stable relations between patients and medical staff. It is precisely within the scope of such local relations that *health care* emerges as a sort of 'side effect' of global trials.

Local relations may be of limited force because a clinical trial must sooner or later come to an end, which may happen only a couple of months after its beginning. However, many trials do last much longer, especially in most advanced phases, such as phase 3. Those which are conducted by a cardiologic hospital in São Paulo, for example, take an average of two years, and may last up to five years.

Oncologic trials, even though they generally involve small numbers of subjects, are the longest ones. As many cancer patients join the study after having tried different drugs, the experience can really be their 'last try', for they generally pass away in the study, three or four years after being recruited. However, when the study focuses on early stages of cancer, participation may last more than ten years. For instance, in 2010 the Spanish private clinical centre I visited was renewing, for two more years, a study that had been initiated in 1998. We are dealing with an example of research subjects receiving *health care* within a trial over 14 years.

In addition, due to various hardships imposed by the disease, oncologists are more likely to stress the therapeutic capacities of clinical studies. Perhaps with a certain amount of exaggeration, Timmermans and Berg (2003, p. 72) claimed: 'Rather than searching for the right patients for the protocol, oncologists often *search the right protocol for their patients…*' This attitude is certainly motivated by the oncologists' professional duties, but it is also worth considering that these duties may be reinforced by personal ties toward patients, which tend to be strong and long-lasting in oncology. In São Paulo, I addressed this issue in an interview with an oncologist:

> *It … seems to me that the relation is more stable in the case of oncology. The patient sees the doctor for a longer period, whereas in other areas, it seems that they change physician more frequently. I don't know if that is correct…*

> *Yes … Hmmm … Generally, yes, the patient remains for a longer period with the oncologist and appointments are very frequent, you know. There are patients who are seen every day. There are patients who are seen at least once a week, you know. You hardly lose contact with a patient for more than one month … So the physician establishes a very close relation to the patient, you know, a very tight linkage…*

It is important to remember that we are not dealing with a marginal side of clinical research. Oncologic trials have constituted the main research focus of pharma companies over the last two decades (Oliveira 1999; Seruga et al. 2010). This trend is also reflected in the activities of the two multinational CROs that participated in my fieldwork. For one of them, oncology is the main area in all the five countries I visited, representing, for instance, about 37 per cent of its studies conducted in France. The other CRO has also important activities in oncology; in South Africa, for example, 30 per cent of its trials focus on cancer.

Thus, as Petryna (2009, p. 8) claimed, the globalization and proliferation of clinical studies is normalizing clinical research, so 'it is rapidly integrated into public health systems and emerging drug markets'. However, there is a phenomenon that has received little attention from different analysts: global trials lead to a new type of *health care* funding, as I claim in the next section.

3.7 Global Trials and 'Disposable Income'

As Santos (1979) points out, whenever a social actor makes a payment, there is another actor who takes the money as income, insofar as this money can be subsequently used to meet everyday costs. In clinical trials, the same phenomenon takes place, even though it does not assume a monetary form. Thanks to the investments made by the trials industry, research subjects are provided with income, for even though they do not receive monetary payments, they receive *health care* without paying for it. In trials, people access *care* without making any expense in terms of taxes (state health system) or fees (private health system). In this way, money can be saved which will increase the monetary amount possessed in the form of what Keynes (2007) called 'disposable income', that is, the sum total of money people have in order to meet everyday costs.

It was shown[7] that in a clinical trial, there are two main monetary flows: reimbursements of hospital costs and payments to research staff. As for reimbursements, the trials industry gives back what it spends. However, it is important to ask what the real fundaments of payments to research teams are. In other words: what are research teams being paid for?

One would immediately feel tempted to claim that these payments remunerate research activities. This reply, which can pop into one's mind in a natural way, sheds some light on the *instrumental* side of trials. However, trials can also be seen from a *communicational* perspective in which the payments received by research teams can be considered to remunerate *health care* activities.

---

7   Section 2.3. See also Figure 2.1.

To be sure, it may sound rather odd to claim that caring activities are performed by clinical research teams, which involve, for instance, data managers who process clinical information or coordinators who deal with regulatory issues. However, this helps us learn another important lesson: *rationalities* also constitute a way to look at the world. The existence of distinct *rationalities* signifies that certain actors can simply despise or ignore factors of paramount relevance for other actors. *Communicational actors* can simply ignore the presence and operations of data managers and research coordinators, in the same way that for a CRO's global manager, there is no need to consider the friendship that emerges between nurses and research subjects during the conduct of a trial.

If an *instrumental* approach to clinical research is used, patients are simply subjects; physicians turn into investigators; and nurses become research nurses. Nevertheless, in the everyday practice of trials, in local contexts, *communicational rationality* emerges and from this point of view, patients are patients again; physicians regain their condition of physicians; and nurses are nothing but nurses. However, such 'inversions' are difficult to realize because we are in the kingdom of *communicational rationality*, whose existence is simply ignored by many analysts.

Different people involved in clinical trials share an underlying assumption: patients go to hospitals to be looked after in the first place, whereas physicians and nurses are based there to provide health care in the first place. This assumption cannot be stripped away at the beginning of a clinical study, simply because it is a deeply embedded social lesson that everyone learns from early ages. In Habermas' (2008, p. 65) terms, we are dealing with 'background knowledge': 'Partners in conversation move within the horizon of an already shared background understanding, even when they must first develop a shared language.'

Even though the assumptions found in background knowledge can be 'forgotten' while remaining effective, they are mobilized whenever one is asked to *justify* the fundaments of an activity (Habermas 2008). In clinical trials, one idea is constantly springing from *background knowledge*: trials are not completely devoid of a *caring* dimension, because they are undertaken in hospitals and conducted by caregivers.

Thus, if payments made to medical staff within a trial has its meaning from an *instrumental* point of view, it must have one from the *communicational* perspective as well, because *rationalities* are also a means to give meaning to the world. From a communicational standpoint, it can be claimed that research teams get paid for the *caring activities* they put in place during a trial. In order to sustain this claim, it is necessary to stress two phenomena.

First, studies' budgets reflect the communicational dimension of payments made to caregivers. Payments made within a trial always depend both on the number of patients recruited and the number of visits and procedures realized. Thus the activity that really triggers the payment is not the hiring of medical staff but the establishment of an actual relationship between the medical staff and the patient.

Second, in our capitalistic, Western, urban societies, provision of health care always implies the use of some funding,[8] which can assume two forms. Health care funding can be shared by the members of a society through the payment of taxes to build up a state health system. Alternatively, health care may be afforded on an individual basis through the hiring of companies and professionals offering private health care activities. In clinical trials, however, a third kind of funding emerges, and this circumstance may be taken into account by physicians and patients. When somebody discusses participation in a clinical trial with a physician, the patient's capacity to afford medicines can be taken into consideration. For example, in a private oncologic practice in São Paulo, a Research Coordinator told me:

> In clinical research, physicians are actually thinking about the patient. If the patient needs the drug and doesn't have money, then it is okay, the physician can refer the patient to another physician [who is running a trial]. But if the patient has the means or has [health] insurance, the physician says: 'Then, we're not going to participate in a clinical trial. We're going to do the normal treatment here, if the drug is already available [on the market], of course.' ... If the patient has the means, it is said: 'No, we're not going to join a clinical study so that I can look after you more closely.'

Thus, whenever medicines can be afforded, the physician would prefer to look after the patient 'more closely'. However, if the person cannot buy expensive medicines, he or she would be referred to another physician who

---

8   I would not oppose the idea that care is not a commodity and, therefore, claiming that it has a monetary value does not make much sense. However, in the framework of capitalism, care (as well as other non-tangible and non-commercial resources such as entertainment or psychological support) has been professionalized and commoditized and, therefore, has become the object of commercial payments.

is conducting a clinical study on the needed compound. In this way, the *health care* provided to the patient would be transferred from normal care to a clinical study. By referring the patient, the physician is not abdicating medical duties but simply changing their location and nature; at the same time, the health care funding is transferred. From the moment when the patient joins the study, he or she will no longer be paying for treatment, and health care will not be guaranteed by the state either. Within a clinical trial, the study's sponsor will assume the costs implied, which includes examinations conducted, medicines taken, and the *caring* attention imparted by the medical staff.[9] This is precisely the socio-economic implication of a physician's affirming that a patient can be referred to a clinical researcher. In a private practice like the one mentioned above, these shifts are easy to see, for it is clear that the patient, once recruited for a trial, ceases to pay for medications and care. In public hospitals, however, these shifts are very subtle insofar as the patient never makes direct payments to caregivers and, therefore, joining a clinical trial seems to have no economic consequences whatsoever.

Previously,[10] I described the monetary flows of clinical trials. In order to complement the scheme, it is possible to schematize the invisible economic relations of global studies:

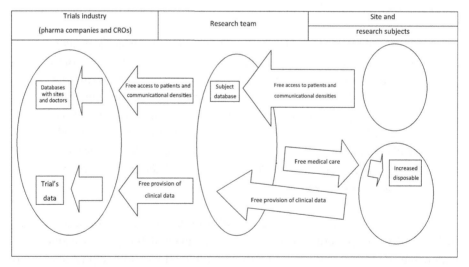

Figure 3.1   Non-monetary, economic exchanges in global world trials

9   However, as was shown in section 2.5, there may be loopholes and some costs of the trial may be surreptitiously transferred to the state.
10   Section 2.3.

As Fisher (2009) explained, by taking part in a clinical study, people must sometimes change their everyday routines. It is necessary to take medications at precise times, visit the site for the study's procedures, and collect accurate information about everyday bodily reactions, sometimes implying filling in long paper or electronic forms. This role that subjects play as providers of huge amounts of clinical information is not remunerated, offsetting the free care they are provided with. By the way, although some companies are eager to claim that people get free medicines in trials, they are silent about the data that companies receive for free from study subjects. Moreover, the trials industry has free access to the *communicational densities* existing at, and canalized by, research sites.[11]

As flows of income within clinical studies take this invisible shape, it is quite difficult to realize their existence. Yet they are very effective at fostering linkages between the different actors involved, as well as producing needs and expectations. For research subjects, access to free care and an increased disposable income eventually leads to an ever-growing need for care and trials.

3.8 The Global Need for Global Trials

Nowadays, in hospitals all over the world, there are vast populations of patients whose health care is assured by the trials industry, a phenomenon that has rather obvious positive aspects, especially if one considers that some promising compounds can be accessed only within clinical studies. However, this situation jeopardizes the research subjects' health security, for it is never certain that research participants will continue to access drugs on completion of trials. As the trials industry becomes 'economically responsible' for some patients for some years, this 'responsibility' may be converted into the 'right of discarding people' at the end of a study.

The proliferation of global trials multiplies the number of people whose disposable income is increased through participation, a phenomenon with two main consequences. First, even though research subjects do not engage in monetary transactions within a trial, the final result of the process (that is, the rise of disposable income) does assume a monetary form because the money saved with health care and medicines is concrete, tangible money. In this way these subjects, by having access to higher amounts of income, can engage

---

11 On this issue, see Chapter 4.

more deeply in everyday monetary relations, therefore being exposed to the rationales triggered by monetary transactions.

> *The money economy enforces the necessity of continuous mathematical operations in our daily transactions. The lives of many people are absorbed by such evaluating, weighing, calculating and reducing of qualitative values to quantitative ones ... Exactness, precision and rigour in the economic relationships in life ... run parallel to the extension of monetary matters... (Simmel 1997, pp. 444–445).*

Second, in urban contexts, money ownership is frequently the password to many activities and possibilities. When their disposable income is increased, individuals have broader access to goods and commodities, which necessarily bring about standards of behaviour and expectations. In this way, individuals plunge into the ethos of an urban lifestyle, within which the need for medicines and modern therapies (and, increasingly, for trials) is one key implication. The expansion of the disposable income, the engagement in urban contexts, and the need for medicines and trials are trends that nourish each other.

As it will be shown in the following chapter, urban *communicational densities* play their role in intensifying the search for trials and the willingness to participate. In this way, the proliferation of global studies amounts to a global increase in the need for trials. Every economist knows that demand and the amount of income are directly related. In clinical trials, the expansion of disposable income (which is possible because people receive *health care* without incurring costs) is leading to an ever-growing demand for medicines and trials. Faced with these pressures, physicians tend to become a greedy crowd that can no longer draw medical *tactics* without taking trials as one of its most crucial *instruments*.

To be sure, participation in trials may have beneficial and effective outcomes for physicians and patients, as illustrated by some examples in this chapter. However, such agreements between physicians and companies will always be burdened by three flaws. First, they are established exclusively by companies and investigators, thus being subject to evident issues of political legitimacy. As Habermas (1996, p. 352) claimed: 'Paragovernmental bargaining arrangements lacking effective ties to the parliamentary complex ... give rise to legitimation problems.'

Second, only the small group of physicians who become key opinion leaders are able to engage in effective negotiations with the trials industry. For the majority of investigators who do not belong to the 'elite of trials', as well as their patients, the special clinical conditions that can be assured through source agreements may be coldly withheld. Thus many potential subjects who would be willing to take part in studies remain at the periphery of clinical research, being kept away from participation. Here, it is possible to repeat Habermas' (1996, p. 350) words: 'Conflicts arise between the neocorporatistically negotiated policies and the constitutional protection of underorganized parts of the population at the periphery of society.'

A third flaw of source agreements is that companies tend to dominate the whole process of negotiations. Even though the industry does concede on some points, a trial is always destined to finish and its result eventually hones the image of the studied medicine. Obviously, companies will be very reluctant to sponsor investigator-initiated studies whose expected results are not favourable to their drugs. Moreover, in any type of trial, it is always uncertain that research subjects will continue to be provided with free medication when studies finish. Thus it is unlikely that source agreements will be 'kept free of illegitimate interventions of social power (i.e., of the factual strength of privileged interests to assert themselves)' (Habermas 1996, p. 150).

In order to cope with such problems, it would be important to bring source agreements from *implicit* arenas to *explicit* forums. *Institutions* can become a space in which investigators and companies discuss their concerns and interests more clearly. In this way, the power of the trials industry could be balanced by the presence of legitimate law. In addition, participation of people in trials that may favour their treatment would no longer be a matter of being 'at the right place at the right time'. Nowadays, patients depend on the concessions that their physicians can get from companies in very particular periods and locations. Moreover, the dynamics of whole cities and countries become subjected to these hidden negotiations of trials, as we shall see in the second part of this book.

PART TWO

Global Trials in the Geographical Space

4

Communication: The Collective Design of Clinical Protocols

In the first part of this book, the installation of global trials into medical institutions was explored. However, hospital and clinics are not independent entities endowed with a separate dynamic. Instead, they draw on the possibilities offered by their places, cities, countries, in a world, their geographical contexts. As we have seen, the trials industry strives to make their global standards function at research sites. In a sense, the same *rationality* applies to geographical spaces, insofar as the features of cities and countries must also be taken into account in the industry's calculations. At the limit, a highly standardized activity implies the formation of the standardized geographical space described by Santos (2000a).

Therefore, from now on we examine the process through which clinical research becomes embedded in local contexts and overlaps with the everyday search for intercomprehension that, according to Habermas (1987), is typical to *communicational rationality*. It is important to point out that when speaking of the geography of trials, we are not simply referring to infrastructures, locations and material resources. As Santos (2000a) explained, the space is composed not only by material infrastructures ('systems of objects') but also by relationships, needs, and inventions ('systems of actions').

In terms of actions, our approach needs to be wisely comprehensive. Because we are dealing with a global activity dominated by multinational actors, it is tempting to ignore the role played by local actors, in particular contexts. According to Will and Moreira (2010, p. 13), 'local groups (patients/professionals) and national actors (governments, regulatory institutions) are also relevant. Here notions of public involvement and public good must be carefully interrogated, and not only through an ethical lens'. Epstein, dealing with the recruitment of research subjects, had already warned us against the emergence of too technical approaches bringing about 'the threat that the issue will be treated as a procedural and technical matter, and that one would forget its complexity in terms of social and personal relations' (Epstein 2007, p. 193).

A comprehensive approach is needed, because if the traditional technical perspective is adopted, one cannot transcend mystifications that are frequent in the universe of global trials. By focusing on the standpoint of local actors, some rigid rationales can be unmasked and questioned. For example, it is known how fiercely and passionately the industry defends its intellectual property rights. These concerns often lead people to speak of protocol design, an activity that is putatively carried out by individual companies. However, we shall see that clinical protocols would not be completely feasible without some inputs and creations offered by local actors. Therefore, the image of an individual protocol-designer prevents us from seeing a process of actual collective design of protocols.

In the present chapter, I claim that the global trials industry would not be successful and effective without paying attention to, and striving to embed its activities into, particular places and socio-geographical contexts. Five phenomena will be studied: the presence of 'communicational densities' in hospitals and medical practices; the use of urban 'communicational densities' by the trials industry; communication between investigators within the so-called 'medical community'; linkages between hospitals in a clinical trial; and the ways in which companies strive to embed their trials into local contexts.

4.1 Research Sites and 'Communicational Densities'

On the walls of hospitals all over the world, if one looks carefully, there are posters announcing clinical studies; something like: 'We are looking for volunteers for a study on diabetes...'. By using such tools, investigators try to speed up the identification and enrolment of research subjects. Some physicians are reluctant to use this strategy because of the distortions it can entail. In fact, it is difficult to make an accurate exposition of a clinical study's purposes and procedures in a few words,[1] therefore some misunderstandings can be provoked. For example, at the lobby of a research centre in São Paulo, I saw a flyer announcing a clinical trial as a 'treatment with a new drug', a description that many ethics committees would be most unwilling to approve.

---

1   In some studies, the information sheet and the informed consent form can have as many as 20 pages.

In spite of possible distortions, announcements in hospitals are surely a powerful way to get participants for studies, especially for relatively common diseases such as diabetes or cardiac illnesses. In an interview with a co-investigator who works in a huge hospital in Madrid, we were talking about the ease and velocity with which her research team recruits patients:

What are the factors that enable the group to be fast?

In fact, we are focused and we gather quickly. And all the means of communication ... Consider that in the hospital there are more than 3,000 workers and there are many patients circulating in the hospital every day. Thus, from the moment you put 15, 20 posters at different points of the hospital, you have many telephone calls [from interested people] in a week. Many. Many.

So the smooth circulation of news within medical sites enables a high recruitment rate. It seems to me that the best concept to interpret this phenomenon was proposed by Santos (2000a): he speaks of *communicational densities*, referring to the fact that in some locations people can engage in personal contacts more easily, sharing knowledge. The concept of *communicational density* leads us a step further from Habermas' lessons, for it enables us to understand that some locations and places are more favourable to, and therefore 'hold more, *communication*' than others.

Hospitals and practices can certainly be seen as settings of high *communicational densities* because they are locations where swift and smooth circulation of news, advice, and messages of several sorts can emerge. As many types of relations happen in those places, it is difficult to establish an actual typology but for the analysis' sake, it would be possible to identify at least three situations in which *communication* takes shape. First, as we have seen, a sort of 'material communication' is verified when investigators decide to use posters or flyers to announce a new study. Second, there are relations between patients and the medical staff, which are an obvious source of *communication* and or trustful relations.[2] For example, the manager of a recruitment centre in London told me that the staff does come to befriend trials volunteers, a fact that can help in the recruitment process of future trials.

There is a third source of communication within hospitals and practices: clinical trials seem to run in a smooth way within a hospital whenever the

---

2   On the role played by trust and hope in the recruitment process, see sections 6.3 and 6.4.

contacts between caregivers are not blocked. On this point, the case of an R&D Coordinator I interviewed in London is illustrative. Communication is what this person's job is all about. She is responsible for supporting the work of physician-investigators based in some hospitals, including the provision of information as well as technical and legal advice so that clinical research can be dealt with more easily by busy caregivers. After a few months in this job, she came to know personally all the hospitals' investigators, being responsible for several types of liaison: people need to be put in touch with the right person in order to get the assistance they are looking for. That is why she pointed out that 'I make sure that everybody is ... in contact with each other so studies run very smoothly.'

Actually, personal contacts are decisive because the establishment of a trial within a hospital involves the diffusion of news and the formation of networks of mutual help. In Madrid, a CRO's Director of Clinical Operations told me:

> once the trial is running, everything depends on the relations the investigator has within the site because if the patient comes through the emergency room, there must be people in the emergency [ward] that agree to participate. The investigator alone can do nothing. There must be people involved within the hospital to help him.

Knowledge of the hospital's characteristics is fundamental because the arrival of a clinical trial must be diffused among people within a department so that everybody can assimilate it, so to speak. As a British Director for Clinical Management described it: 'there will be networking in the hospital like in the word of mouth'. In other cases, people working at the hospital, having heard about a trial being conducted there, can even try to become research subjects, becausethe hospital's staff also sees posters that are spread within the hospital and can volunteer to participate.

These flows of communication are sometimes acknowledged and explored by the trials industry. For example, a Spanish CRO's Director for Clinical Management declared that in Spain a study is, in most cases, proposed to the chair of the hospital's department and this person would indicate colleagues who might be interested in running the study. The CRO avoids contacting physicians directly, and therefore circumventing the chair's control, because 'in Spain hierarchy is quite important'. Thus it is necessary to acknowledge not only institutional but also regional or national traditions.

In hospitals, the trials industry is obviously successful at finding both skilled investigators (Fisher 2009; Petryna 2009) and bodies for experimentation (Angell 2005; Shah 2006; Epstein 2007; Fisher 2009; Petryna 2009). However, it is important to draw attention to another search, which happens in a more surreptitious way: the search for *communicational densities*. Indeed, hospitals are important for the trials industry also because they hold rich flows of *communication* without which clinical studies would wither at their very initial phase. After being approved, and before being conducted, clinical trials must be *communicated* in concrete research sites. Moreover, communication taking place in cities can also be very helpful, as we see in the next section.

4.2 Clinical Trials in Urban Contexts

As I said elsewhere (Bicudo 2011), the global trials industry is always looking for urban contexts, a phenomenon that has not been sufficiently stressed by many analysts. Indeed, cities, and especially the largest ones, constitute favourable contexts for companies wishing to conduct global studies. In urban contexts the circulation of news and the frequency of personal contacts are intensified. In other words, it is possible to consider the city as a place of social diversity, frequent relations and high *communicational densities*. 'The big city is a huge common space, the most meaningful of places. Within it, all capitalistic enterprises, all types of work, all technical and organizational forms can find some leeway for establishment, coexistence and prosperity' (Santos 2000b, p. 322).

Means of communication and systems of transport are more sophisticated in cities as opposed to areas of lower technical development. People, goods and news circulate more quickly and efficiently, in flows that are fostered by an intense division of social labour (Durkheim 1932). Clinical trials are one of many activities to benefit from the smooth flows of communication made possible by urban contexts. Theoretically, the bigger the city, the more probable the identification and enrolment of participants for trials will be. In São Paulo, I interviewed a Clinical Manager of a private trials centre. He had worked for a similar centre in Buenos Aires, Argentina, and I asked him to compare those cities.

> *Would you say that, when it comes to clinical research, São Paulo is a more dynamic city [than Buenos Aires]?*

> *There are more patients available [in São Paulo], which makes the options of treatment much more interesting for volunteers ... Illnesses*

of a low occurrence, in a population that has two million, three million, four million inhabitants, do occur, but they seldom occur. In a city that has eleven million inhabitants, they appear much more frequently. It is easier to find a person, per square metre, with rheumatoid arthritis in São Paulo than in Buenos Aires because there are more people here.[3]

São Paulo, the main economic hub of Brazil and one of the biggest cities in the world, certainly attracts the trials industry's interest. In an interview conducted there with a Research Coordinator of a cardiologic hospital, we were talking about the big number of potential research subjects in the city:

It is many people. A city with 20 million inhabitants, it is enough for any site, I think ... I know a hospital that has many studies on dermatology. They finish [the recruitment] in seconds. There are waiting lists to participate in studies ... There was a course on clinical research [in the hospital she is based in] and some external staff came to give classes and talks, and they used to say: 'Gee we have waiting lists! People want to participate when there is [a trial on] an anti-wrinkle cream.' There are queues! If there is an anti-ageing cream, they close the [recruitment] list in two seconds.

However, the size of the population is never the only criterion that determines a city's suitability for clinical trials. In addition to the population they hold, big cities often concentrate rare services and therefore attract a population living close to, or even very far from them (Bicudo 2011). Once again, São Paulo is a good example. The city took the lead in the Brazilian economy as early as the 1930s, and its predominance has increased throughout the decades. As a result, many activities have been concentrated in São Paulo, including health care services. Key hospitals have been installed in here, attracting patients who come from all over the huge Brazilian territory. Thus the recruitment potential of São Paulo's hospitals goes much beyond the official city's area.

The geography of a city, which may turn it into a medical, touristic or economic hub, may be decisive for the trials industry's purposes. In cities such as London, Madrid, Paris, Johannesburg or São Paulo, the gathering of different types of companies, operating in different domains, may at any moment become interesting from the trials industry's point of view. For instance, CROs

---

3   In Buenos Aires, there are about 12 million inhabitants whereas in São Paulo this number is nearer 20 million. In both cases, we are considering not only the city itself but also adjacent areas receiving the direct economic influence of the main city.

often hire translation services, because documents such as research contracts and consent forms must be translated into the local language. In big cities, companies offering cheap translation services can be easily found and hired. Another example is the presence of laboratories for clinical tests, which can be rapidly found in big cities and become CROs' partners.

However, it is crucial to talk about a deeper, more decisive feature in the geography of cities. In those places, *communicational densities* can reach very high degrees, and the abundance of personal contacts and flows of news becomes a factor of paramount relevance for clinical trials. In Porto Alegre, for example, I interviewed a CRO's Manager for Clinical Operations who had previously worked as a monitor. She told me that the personal contacts she had established in her previous position helped her to negotiate and liaise with sites in her new function. Indeed, monitors are the main professionals to participate in this flow of *communication* with sites. As a result, a CRO can be put in contact with new investigators whenever it hires monitors from other companies.

The trials industry's activities are facilitated not only by the relations between the industry's employees and the research sites' staff. Social contacts between research subjects can also have an astonishing multiplying effect. In São Paulo, for example, the Clinical Manager of a private centre for clinical studies told me:

> *Do you know what my biggest source [of participants] is today? One patient comes here, joins a clinical trial or tries to join a clinical trial, he is received very well and he indicates [the centre] to his friends. 'Go there, they receive you very nicely, they are very good, they take care of you properly, they will listen to you and try to help you, go there...' They call us and fix an appointment.*

Thus research subjects spontaneously become sources of information, referring friends to clinical research sites. Surprisingly, South Africa was the only country where this phenomenon was not strongly stressed by my interviewees. This is possibly due to the inheritances of the apartheid era, which imposed several types of fragmentations to South African cities. In spite of the lively and dynamic configuration of these urban contexts, the circulation of news and people continues to be quite limited. Another factor is spoken communication itself in this country with eleven official languages. Even though a fair amount of the national population does speak English, everyday contacts and the formation of social groups are, in most cases, mediated by other languages and dialects. Indeed, South Africa is a country where one can take a train for a long journey and hear a different language by entering a different coach.[4]

In the other countries I studied, however, the relevance of personal messages between research subjects was frequently highlighted by my interviewees. In Paris, for example, a physician who is based in a key hospital told me: 'Subjects phone us very often because they know, because a friend has told them that there is a study…' At the outset of trials, when participants must be looked for, this task can therefore be facilitated by the *communicational densities* of cities, where the establishment of a trial can be rapidly communicated among people.

Another advantage of urban contexts is that patients with the same disease can gather in *spontaneous* or formal groups. Epstein (1996), for instance, showed the relevant role played by HIV activist groups in the 1980s. It is known that sick people sometimes share experiences and advice within formal associations, which can become environments for the circulation of news about trials. A psychologist who works in a clinic for smoking-related diseases in London gives us another interesting example:

> *Smokers usually know smokers. So if they've had a good experience [with trials in the clinic] and they've managed to stop [smoking], they usually end up telling their friends and family about how they've stopped. And so, you know, you quite often get friends of friends and family members that come through, so … Yeah. Word of mouth. Oh, you get the same at the trials recruitment as well because someone will sign up, so: 'Oh, I've got somebody in the office that I might get to call and get some information.' So it works, kind of, in the recruitment as well … You know, somebody that really wants to stop smoking, they've usually got a friend that really wants to stop smoking as well, so … And it is always good for them to do it together. You can, kind of, go through the process with a bit more of support.*

Here we are also dealing with an issue of time. The trials industry is concerned not only with finding research subjects but also finding them as quickly as possible. However, the *spontaneous communication* that is analysed in this chapter does not occur in the way that the industry wishes. Personal

---

4   Another particularity of South Africa is the important presence of foreigners in trials. The country attracts large migratory flows from other African countries, and these people have been grasping the opportunity to register in South African hospitals, which seem not to present major barriers or strict criteria.

contacts, from the viewpoint of multinational companies, happen at a quite slow pace, because they depend on cultural aspects and personal preferences. In addition, companies cannot shape and manage the configuration of the cities' communicational features. In this way, although *communicational densities* do benefit the trials industry's activities, a temporal mismatch emerges. For slow, uncertain personal contacts take place while companies are always in a hurry and looking for greater controllability.

In order to minimize such impasses, companies, by means of ingenious tools, may try to *induce* events that would otherwise take place in a slow manner. In Pretoria, for example, a private clinical trials centre, when facing difficulties to find participants for a study, may call some people registered in its database and ask for indications of relatives and/or friends. Another example was obtained in a private recruitment centre in London. People who take part in a clinical trial can fill in a referral form, which was elaborated for them to indicate potential participants. If the indication is successful (that is, if the indicated person does come to join a study in the centre), a payment is made to the person who makes the indication. In this case, the company simply does not wait for *spontaneous communication* between participants to happen; instead, it *induces* it by means of 'referral forms' and small payments. The Clinical Trials Administrator of this centre told me that 'quite a lot of people do refer'. So it is possible to conclude that the company manages to speed up the *communicative* process and exercise some amount of control over the *communicational densities* of its urban environment.

It is always useful to remember that *communication* cannot be reduced to the use of verbal messages. In talking about *communication*, I am referring to every process and product that helps to associate actions of different actors, promoting or facilitating the 'search for intercomprehension' which is pointed out by Habermas (1987). However, when it comes to the everyday life of ordinary people who often lack sophisticated skills and technical tools, *communication* frequently does imply the use of verbal language and simple interpersonal messages. Thus we can only find it significant when the administrator of this recruitment centre affirms that 'we do get, you know, quite a lot of response from word of mouth in various different sources'.

The *mediational action* plays an important role here by offering a social and geographical reference to social actors. Every day people hear about clinical studies, and this novelty is often heard about in the form of 'somewhere to go'. If the trials industry and research subjects manage to meet, this is possible because there are *mediational actions* being undertaken in precise locations (hospitals, clinics and research centres).

Due to the intervention of *mediational actions*, the trials industry has access to the *communicational densities* of urban contexts. The *mediational action* is providing the trials industry with communication, one of the most precious resources of local contexts. Thus, even in those situations where clinical trials are not announced in advertisement campaigns, companies manage to successfully identify research subjects. From a sociological standpoint, personal contacts, social relations, mutual help, in a nutshell *communication* is the most precious discovery that the trials industry has ever managed to realize.

Nowadays, in many countries, people go to hospitals in the hope of being put into a clinical study. This was said by a co-investigator interviewed in Madrid:

> **And these are people who phone, who come ...**
>
> *Yes, they come. News circulates among them, they tell each other. Those who have participated in some studies tell their friends, neighbours, relatives, and ... they come: 'Whenever you do a study on overweight, on obesity, take me into account.' Thus we take note of all their data and we make this database with all those people who are interested in participating in this kind of study.*

In this Spanish hospital, a subject database has therefore been created. It is an informational tool with which this research team can grasp and solidify the flows of communication that cross the hospital every day. Across the world, many similar databases are formed with volunteers who look for clinical trials.[5]

Apparently, clinical trials have been fostering fragmentations within hospitals. Such databases express this phenomenon, for their formation is always up to separate research teams that would never share this information with other teams. However, as we shall see in the following sections, there are also frequent contacts and flows of communication between research teams and hospitals, a phenomenon that can also prove beneficial for companies looking for research subjects.

---

5   These databases also belong to the invisible economic relations of trials. Therefore, they are depicted in Figure 3.1.

4.3 The Medical Community

We have seen[6] that clinical trials are frequently *communicated* within hospitals. The networks defined by clinical research go beyond the borders of particular sites. Actually, it would be fair to say that clinical studies, more than being simply conducted in hospitals, are installed in cities.

If one looks exclusively at the trials industry, one might have the impression of separate sites operating independently. Nevertheless, when we draw attention to what happens in the actual recruitment process, it becomes clear that hospitals and practices must cooperate in order to meet the trials industry's rigid deadlines. Referral networks involving specialists in the same disease can be used to facilitate recruitment (Mueller 1997). Whenever a research team faces difficulties in recruiting research subjects, it may seek for help from other teams. A French paediatrician who is based in a Centre for Clinical Investigation (CIC) gave me an example:

> **Is there communication between the CIC and other CICs of other hospitals?**
>
> *Yes, sure ... For instance, in Paris there are four paediatric hospitals ... I conducted, with colleagues of my hospital, a certain number of studies for which we did not have the recruitment that had been anticipated. In that moment, I simply phoned my colleagues in another hospital where there is a CIC, in order to ask them if they would accept to take part in the study and in this manner we could complete the recruitment.*

Equally, a research team can refer subjects to another team. That is useful because in some studies, the number of participants to be included in each site is decided upon at the beginning and must be strictly respected. A Research Coordinator who works in an oncologic practice in São Paulo said:

> *We have partnerships with other sites. Actually, it is only a means of communication. So if I am conducting a study here and there is no more places in the study ... I can include only eight patients here and this number of patients is achieved and we find another patient here who wants to join the study, what can I do? I look for another site (which is often the closest hospital to me) and I call them to say: 'Are you also*

---

6   Section 4.1.

> *conducting that study with that sponsor?' ... If they say yes, I refer the*
> *patient to be treated there.*

Therefore, *spontaneous communication* between research sites can be really beneficial to the trials industry. What is more, these relations frequently take place in a smooth way because even though they do not work in the same hospital, physicians often see each other at conferences and medical events. Thus friendships can be established which may subsequently foster the 'flow of participants' within a clinical study.

As we pointed out elsewhere (Almeida and Bicudo 2010), medical events have been used by pharma companies in order to establish lasting relations with physicians and diffuse ideas and expectations relating to medicine and therapy. By the same token, when a company wants to initiate a clinical study, something about the trial may be published strategically at a congress. According to a CRO's monitor interviewed in Madrid:

> *Generally, we [monitors] arrive in the site in a condition that many of*
> *the investigators already know that the compound [to be tested] exists.*
> *They say: 'Oh, have you come to present me that project which is being*
> *conducted by Roche?' They have heard in a congress that Roche is*
> *going to initiate an investigation in Europe on that ... The majority of*
> *investigators already know what we are talking about...*

Sometimes, after hearing about a study in a medical event, physicians may even approach the CRO to try to join it. Even more shrewdly, the company can ask an opinion leader[7] to spread the future conduct of the trial among his or her colleagues. In this way, physicians who are based in different sites can become willing to participate in the promising trial.

Therefore, the personal relationships between physicians can be turned into an economic tool. In São Paulo, another monitor remembered quite curious stories:

> **Have you realized if there is any site or any investigator that is**
> **faster at recruiting patients?**
>
> *They sometimes, as they all know each other ... So you go to a medical*
> *population, everybody is a neurologist. They start a competition among*

---

7   On the role played by opinion leaders in trials, see section 3.1.

them. So they are friends and they provoke each other. This happened in a study on an infectious disease. 'Look, I'm going to put more patients than you.' 'No, forget it. I'm going to put more.' And they carried on. And they called each other. 'Oh, I recruited one patient today.' 'Oh, I recruited two last week' ...

And that ends up being good for you?

It is excellent for us. And sometimes we can even stimulate that. So once there was a period in which there were only two countries in the study: Brazil and Argentina. In the period of the Football World Cup. And we sent emails to physicians to say: 'Look, Brazil has this amount [of patients recruited] and Argentina has this amount' [laughter]. And so it began. They began to recruit patients crazily.

Thus flows of *communication* connecting research sites favour the trials industry's strategies. In some cases in which such *communicational densities* reach higher degrees, an investigational culture can emerge. For example, as a French physician explained to me, the physician-investigators based in the central part of Paris are responsible for about 10 per cent of research conducted in the country.

And why?

It is the configuration. Actually there are 867 researchers here, physician-investigators ... There is pressure, there is permanent pressure. We are called: 'Are you available? Can you help to do a budget and submit a proposal? Can you help on that?' We are always under pressure. So that gives us the willingness to do research.

Under pressure from whom?

Pressure from physician-investigators, from physicians who have ideas and come to talk to us: 'Oh, there is a call for proposals. Can you help me?' ... We are constantly stimulated.

What this investigator names 'pressure' is approximately what, from a sociological standpoint, I am proposing to frame with the concept of *communicational density*. As he clearly expressed, the easiness with which investigators can get in touch, spread news and do mutual invitations leads to the production of a research environment which is *spontaneously* formed and can be subsequently explored by the trials industry.

From the very first interviews I conducted with investigators and research coordinators, the hazards leading people to clinical trials intrigued me. I had the impression that people are falling into the universe of trials 'by chance'. In different countries, there is a dearth of courses and degrees in clinical trials, leading people to learn the intricacies of clinical research through their own effort and personal experience. As a result, talking to someone or being invited by someone are common ways through which professionals are enrolled for working with trials. From a student who is put into a clinical study by his or her supervisor to a jobseeker who hears about a job opportunity in a research site, people are being recruited for clinical research thanks to the intervention of most effective *communicational densities*.

In clinical trials *communication* is not only a tool that enables the identification of professionals for technical operations; it is rather a powerful social phenomenon that pervades the whole system, going from global companies to local contexts. The fact that *communication* is not restricted to particular sites but can cross institutional borders is another evidence that enables us to talk about an action, a *mediational action*. Indeed, we are not simply dealing with personal characteristics and skills of certain researchers. Even though some investigators do have greater ability to establish relationships and therefore engage in efficient recruitment networks, the existence of *communication* within clinical trials goes beyond personal talents, being a widespread event, which I could identify in different institutions and countries.

Bourdieu's (1989) concept of 'social capital' might be evoked here. As Bordieu did, I am talking about the fact that individuals liaise and establish different sorts of relationships. However, unlike Bourdieu, I am not referring to opportunities that individuals glean from those relationships. With the ideas of *communication* and communicational density, it is possible to go beyond individual capacities and achievements in order to focus on the features of places and activities. From this point of view, it can be said that the global trials industry is not threatened by, but rather benefits from, the particularities of social relations taking place at the local scale. *Communication* is everywhere a necessary aspect of global trials, without which the enterprise would never have its current configuration and success.

4.4 Where do Research Subjects Really Come From?

There is another *complementary* process in clinical trials. On the one hand, the trials industry treats investigators and investigative sites as autonomous players. For example, as we have seen,[8] recruitment efforts are dealt with on an individual basis, each investigator being monetarily rewarded by his or her numbers. On the other hand, by focusing on the actual ways in which recruitment works, it is quite clear that physicians and medical centres are far from working separately. On the contrary, the networks analysed in the previous section are pivotal structures by means of which recruitment targets can be reached. As a Global Director for Patient Recruitment explained to me, physician-investigators contacted by CROs often indicate colleagues to work in clinical trials. He said that his company can put advertisements on the Internet in order to identify researchers for a study; 'there are various channels where you can advertise, but by far and away the best source is referral and word of mouth'.

Thus, even though the trials industry has a fragmented approach at the global scale, the actual organization of trials, at the local scale, follows collective patterns. As a psychologist working in a research team in London stressed, 'clinics work together'. In some cases, physicians can even look for a clinical trial for their patients to be put in. This is the explanation of a physician working in a private research centre in Madrid:

> Sometimes a doctor receives a patient with a certain disease and knows that there is a hospital in a close province running this clinical trial. He or she tries the best so that the patient can participate in that trial. However, it must be a very particular case in which there is nothing very clearly established because in Spain it is difficult to refer patients from a hospital to another.

Communication may have such a *spontaneous* form but in other cases, it can manifest itself in a more organized way. For example, a Research Coordinator working in a key state hospital in Porto Alegre formulated an electronic newsletter that is sent to other medical institutions. In this way, she can let many research teams know about studies being conducted by her research team. Since launching its newsletter, this research team has managed to enhance its recruitment performance, sometimes enrolling patients coming from distant cities. What is interesting is that the newsletter is sent not only to state hospitals

---

8   Section 1.5.

but also to private ones. In this way, patients who are receiving health care in a private hospital can end up being recruited for a clinical trial in a state hospital. The principal investigator of this research team also works in a private hospital that is also located in Porto Alegre. In this way, he can not only transfer research subjects from the state to the private hospital but also the other way around. Thus, on the one hand, the *communicative flows* of clinical trials are blurring the frontiers between state and private hospitals. On the other hand, it really seems appropriate to temper the discourse when conveying the existence of isolated investigators and sites.[9]

If flows of communication can be both *spontaneous* and *organized*, they can also be *induced* by the trials industry, which can ask for indications and referrals. According to a British Director of Clinical Management:

> *If we are doing a study, say diabetes, we go to the diabetes people*
> *[physicians] and say: 'Look, we need more sites, you know, cause this*
> *is a difficult study to recruit.' And there are general recommendations.*
> *They nominate other people they know do research in the area.*[10]

Once again, we are dealing with an issue of time. *Spontaneous* indications of researchers do occur, but they may take time to happen. When CROs *induce* the process, it becomes quicker and more subject to their control. Thus the interplay between global and local actions, which is possible thanks to the role played by *mediational actions*, tends to submit local relations to a new time frame. Even though such relations will never be as rapid as global actions, they are nevertheless put to work in a new rhythm that is more in tune with global companies' purposes.

To summarize, it seems inaccurate to say that research teams and sites are recruiting research subjects independently. A research coordinator of a private oncologic practice in Porto Alegre told me that in the city, 'everybody recruits from everybody'. This is really a precise portrait of the dynamics of

---

9 In São Paulo, I attended a conference organized by the Brazilian Society for Professionals of Clinical Research (*Sociedade Brasileira de Profissionais em Pesquisa Clínica*). At this event I met some research coordinators from different sites of Porto Alegre, both government and private ones. They had all travelled together from Porto Alegre to São Paulo to attend the conference.

10 In Spain, a CRO's Director for Clinical Management did almost the same description: 'Another source to know new investigators is to ask to investigators: "We are going to do a study in this specialty, we propose you to participate. Can you indicate some other sites or investigators that you consider that may work on this specialty or may see this kind of patients?" So they sometimes do recommendations.'

clinical trials all over the world. As we have seen, investigators and sites are in permanent contact, thereby forming recruitment networks. Research subjects may be referred not only from one city to another but can also cross the border separating private and state hospitals. As a result, instead of suggesting that the trials industry recruits participants in hospitals and practices, it is arguably wiser to say that recruitment happens in cities and regions. If this socio-geographical heart of clinical research does not beat, global trials are sentenced to death. In the following section, we shall look at some strategies the trials industry marshals in order to activate this underlying dimension of clinical research.

4.5 Global Trials Embedded in Local Contexts

As a student or staff member of a London College, one receives emails from time to time in which clinical trials are circulated. Investigators are always looking for volunteers to take part in studies on various diseases and conditions. If one takes the time to read some of the proposed methods of clinical study, some projects sound quite interesting to join. This vague, almost inconsequential feeling can become the source of participation in a clinical study.

Inspiring such willingness is precisely what many people, not only in the trials industry but also in medical sites and universities, struggle to do. In some countries, such as the United States, advertisements for clinical trials are as common as various other campaigns. Magazines, posters, brochures, radio, television and other media are commonly used. In other countries, such as France, the trials industry is trying its very first steps toward the formation of an advertisement culture, while in countries such as Brazil, the allowance of large campaigns to circulate trials seems to be a distant reality.

Even though the UK does not repeat the approach of the United States, advertisements have been used in order to circulate some clinical studies. For instance, the recruitment centre I visited in London has already put posters in tube stations, finding many research subjects. The clinic for smoking-related diseases I visited also uses newspapers across London to circulate its studies. The Manager of the Trials Unit of a Hospital in London talked about some precautions to be taken when using advertisements:

> Quite often you have to be quite careful about, if you're doing an advertising campaign, where you actually put the advert because

you've got to think about who the audience is but also what their access is likely to be and what their desire is likely to be. So if you don't bear those in mind, then you can do an advertising campaign and get no response at all.

Not surprisingly, this sounds like marketing advice. In the same way that marketing campaigns aim to embed certain products into the everyday life of a group, advertisements of clinical trials try to *embed* certain studies into specific contexts. As we have seen, effective recruitment activities depend on *communicative flows* taking place between investigators, study coordinators, investigative sites, and potential research subjects. In a word, every clinical study must be *communicated* in order to be adequately established. Whenever the trials industry, or the carriers of *mediational actions* within a research site, manages to launch a successful advertisement campaign for a trial, *communicative densities* are awaked, leading to favourable recruitment performances.

The Internet has widened such possibilities, for it has made it easier to circulate the conduct of studies in some websites. Some CROs are already trying to develop tools in order to explore these capacities. Activities such as the identification of research subjects, advertisements of trials and the search for doctors who see many patients with a particular disease, are beginning to be conducted on the Internet. Even though such strategies are still at an early phase, they are likely to be strengthened in the years to come as a result of the companies' efforts and the expansion of Internet itself.

Then, the trials industry and research teams are, in a sense, realizing that recruiting research subjects requires adaptations to the everyday life of places and social groups. It would be useless to undertake recruitment activities that were in line with sophisticated clinical and scientific methods but at odds with local customs and practices. A beautiful example was given by a psychologist who works in the research team of a clinic for smoking-related diseases in London:

Does it often take much time [to recruit research subjects]?

I think last time we recruited ... Last year we did one ... It was 120 people ... And how we tend to do the screening sessions is to do it on the weekend just to make it accessible for everyone. Over the Saturday and the Sunday. I think we've got 120 in two weekends. One of the reasons for this pace is that the study had straightforward exclusion criteria.

For this particular study, the research team had initially put some advertisements on newspapers. Subsequently, as the interviewee explained, screening sessions[11] were conducted on the weekend. It is interesting that the interviewee seemed to be unaware of the astonishing recruitment performance of her team, which recruited 40 subjects per day, in average. Obviously, it was a wise decision to avoid working days, when most people would simply drop the sessions for their jobs' sake. This is an example of an adjustment in which the characteristics of urban life are taken as the framework in which trials activities are conducted.

In Pretoria, I was given another example by the Managing Director of a private recruitment organization, a company that is hired either by CROs or pharma companies to realize both the recruitment of patients and the conduct of some of the studies' procedures. This company has two sites, the first one located close to the centre of Pretoria, in a place with an affluent population, whereas the second site is situated in a poor area, or a 'black area' as the interviewee referred to it. For this poor area, the company has found an ingenious strategy for identifying research subjects. Nurses are hired to approach people in their homes or public locations, in order to talk about clinical trials and register people who would be interested in joining a study. Language is an issue here, because the area is inhabited by people with different native languages, so the nurses must be able to communicate in these languages, in addition to English and Afrikaans. As far as the interviewee knows, South Africa is the only country where this strategy is used:

> *Because it works for us and it is not too expensive, you know, to employ a nurse on a part time basis to go out and go and find patients, whereas in the UK it would be very expensive ... We have found this to be probably our most successful patient recruitment model, to actually send people to go and talk to people about recruitment or getting them involved in clinical studies...*

Once again, the establishment of a successful recruitment strategy depended on an ability to grasp the main social features of an area. In South Africa, some people have precarious and infrequent access to official health services, and some are bound to traditional healing customs. These characteristics may prevent potential research subjects from being identified in medical institutions. The aforementioned strategy implemented by the recruitment organization is

---

11   Initial examinations that are made to verify whether people fit the inclusion and exclusion criteria of a study.

aimed at circumventing these difficulties by sending emissaries who talk to people in a friendly and understandable way, attracting their attention toward clinical trials.

So far we have dealt with studies in which it is necessary to recruit individuals. However, in some trials, consent must be obtained not only from the research subject but also, or exclusively, from the group of people that is closely attached to the subject. That is what happens, for instance, in trials on neurology, in which the research subject is not capable of assessing the consequences of participation, and people who are responsible for him or her must take the decision. Another example is paediatrics, in which the child does not fully understand the study and parents must consent to participation. These are situations in which the ability to recruit goes beyond the comprehension of one's desires and characteristics, reaching the realm of family traditions and local relations.

In order to foster recruitment performances, trials companies are beginning to use systematic studies about social relations and geographical features. Epstein (2007, pp. 182–183) identified the birth of a new discipline that he called 'recruitmentology':

> *Increasingly, recruitmentologists are developing an empirical body of studies scientifically evaluating the efficacy of various social, cultural, psychological, technological, and economic means of convincing people ... that they want to become, and remain, human subjects.*

However, all this 'recruitmentological' set of information must be complemented by personal skills whose effectiveness escapes the domain of written studies. As the Managing Director of a private trials centre in Pretoria precisely claimed, recruitment 'is an art. It is not only a science, it is an art as well.' People recruiting and doing research on trials participants must surely comply with global standards but: 'Working with standards does not imply that staff members' activities become more machinelike or mechanized ... Rather, we have observed highly skilful and creative activities in the interactions with standards' (Timmermans and Berg 2003, p. 76).

The examples invoked in this section signal that the waves of economic activities continue to mingle with social relations, a trend that was described by Polanyi (1944, p. 219): 'Briefly, the strain sprang from the zone of the market; from there it spread to the political sphere, thus comprising the whole of society.'

To be sure, the trials industry has reached a phase of advanced globalization. However, this achievement does not imply that global actions can now be undertaken without relying on relationships and expertise that can only be manifested at the local level. In order to further explore this phenomenon, we address, in the following section, the issue of amendments to clinical protocols.

4.6 What is a Protocol's Amendment?

Every multinational trial begins with the design of a clinical protocol, a task that in the vast majority of cases is undertaken by either a pharmaceutical company or a CRO. 'Clinical trial protocols are, at least in the ideal, templates for action: they define the terms and conditions of the investigation and, by extension, they guide the activities and practices of clinical trial workers' (Mueller 1997, p. 67).

In theory, thus, these documents would be expressions of the industry's scientific accuracy. However, it is on this very point that the industry's precision shows its limitations. Sometimes, companies are not fully capable of defining the most suitable inclusion and exclusion criteria for a study. Because they lack the clinical expertise that hospitals concentrate, they may conceive unrealistic criteria. The solution to this problem is once again the conduct of feasibility studies.[12] As a French Feasibility Manager told me, the feedback companies have from sites during the process is extremely valuable:

> *The purpose of a feasibility [study] is also to improve the protocol. The protocol, when we receive it for a feasibility [study], is not yet closed. Then, the interest is precisely to have an answer, a feedback from sites, which may say: 'This selection criterion is not suitable at all; it will avoid us recruiting patients.' And we will try to draw the [sponsor's] attention by saying: 'Be careful with this criterion. If it is kept, there will be very few patients put into this study.'*

Thus, the initial version of clinical protocols may present criteria that are not realistic or practical. These frailties go up from research sites to the sponsor, as described by a South African Clinical Manager based in a multinational CRO:

> *Sometimes, they [criteria] are too stringent, because medicines aren't an exact science and you're operating with the whole set of variables,*

---

12   See section 1.3.

and they may change from country to country. And sometimes the investigators do say that they think that the inclusion criteria are too stringent; they won't get this patient because this is the perfect patient. So, for instance, they want a patient ... (that happens, often, in the pain studies in South Africa) they want patients who have pain, like neuropathic pain, but a lot of our patients who get pain (neuropathic pain) are HIV positive. So they exclude HIV positive patients from the study, and then they don't get patients; then, they realize they're not getting patients; then, they amend the protocol to include HIV positive patients, so that they can increase their population base.

In São Paulo, the Research Coordinator of an oncologic practice declared: 'I've been receiving protocols that don't have precise inclusion criteria. And so we have to call the sponsor so that they explain and they have to make amendments.'

In clinical research, an amendment is a modification made to the protocol, so that difficulties can be addressed, such as the dearth of suitable participants. Every member of an ethics committee knows very well that companies often change the strategies and methodologies initially proposed in their protocols. Amendments are so common in the universe of global trials that Chow (2011) recommended that regulatory agencies should formulate more stringent rules about this practice, limiting its occurrence.

Another example is the so-called 'investigator meeting', which takes place before the beginning of a trial, when all research sites have been selected. The investigators who will take part in the trial, and sometimes also their research coordinators, are invited to a meeting that is organized by either the study's sponsor or the CRO. A kind of course is then provided, so that those professionals can be taught the appropriate procedures and standards they will have to comply with in the trial. As a Brazilian Research Coordinator of an oncologic practice explained to me, investigator meetings offer an opportunity for physicians to help improve a protocol:

To physicians, as they have very tight time frames, the meeting is good because it is the place where they can say what the troubles are going to be at recruiting patients and conducting the study ... in the meeting, depending on some aspects of the protocol, they are really willing to say: 'Look, this strategy is fine, that strategy is not fine. I am telling you

from now that, of ten patients I could recruit, I will manage to recruit
four. Why? Because you're limiting the population to join the study.

This is another crucial feature of the *mediational action* that is undertaken at research sites: it can provide global actors with the view of local contexts without which the *instrumental action* would simply crumble in the middle of economic and scientific concerns. Between the statistic targets of *instrumental actors* and the medical features of concrete places, the mediational action associates domains that would otherwise lack any kind of dialogue.

Every day, protocols are designed by the scientific boards of pharma companies or CROs; analysed by ethics committees; proposed to investigators; submitted to national regulatory agencies; mentioned in scientific publications. One might suppose that we are dealing with very precise and strict documents. However, by accompanying the trajectory of protocols, it is clear that their final configuration can derive from many adjustments and negotiations between the industry and investigators. Timmermans and Berg (2003, pp. 72–73) are thus right to say: 'A protocol, after all, only does something when it is picked up, interpreted, acted upon, and passed on…' Research protocols, instead of being rigid documents deriving from accurate scientific rules, are unstable products of uncertain processes in which *validity* is the prevailing rule.

Furthermore, it is at the local scale that a clinical protocol's viability is concretely assessed. For without having some feedback from research teams, the trials industry might be designing unrealistic, clumsy protocols that might never be put into practice. Without such feedback, amendments and corrections to protocols would be much less frequent in the world of clinical research. Therefore, the 'feasibility' of a clinical study is gauged not only through the CROs' 'feasibility forms' but also through the everyday test undergone by every multinational trial when it is embedded in concrete sites and places.

4.7 The Collective Design of Clinical Protocols

In the first chapter of this book, I argued that the construction of an abstract space was one of the biggest feats of the trials industry. By means of the global diffusion of several standards, it has been possible to produce many types of *commensurable* things that can be compared in order to display the safety and efficacy of new drugs (Timmermans and Berg 2003; Lakoff 2005). In this chapter, however, we came across many examples that speak of quite opposite phenomena. Everywhere we look, particular relations, specific needs, local characteristics, in a world *incommensurable* events call our attention. Global actors have to allow the existence of local creations and relations while looking after the overall coherence of their data, products and publications.

> *A key challenge then is finding ways to talk about and acknowledge the difficulties of producing credible evidence, and ways to get trials to carry information about their conditions of production away from the research site, and into journals, policy documents, guidelines and consulting rooms (Will and Moreira 2010, p. 13).*

It is possible to claim that this challenge has been growing bigger and bigger over the last years. On the one hand, there is an ever-increasing need for *commensurables*, because studies on new drugs have multiplied. On the other hand, at the very same moment in which one tries to conduct an accurate and standardized clinical trial, it is necessary to rely on a myriad of facts and phenomena whose features escape the controllability searched for by global companies. In this way, believing too fiercely in the precision and objectivity of the inudstry's products (medicines, publications, figures, among others) would amount to self-delusion. According to Porter:

> *Every scientific result begins its career as a view from somewhere – say some particular laboratory – and it is really the most fundamental task of every scientist to transform as much as possible into a view from nowhere, at least nowhere in particular (1992, pp. 646–647).*

Global clinical research is always laden with 'nowheres' and 'somewheres'. However, these 'somewheres' (*communicational rationality*) are no longer simple laboratories: they are concrete hospitals, cities and countries, which are engraving their marks on the surface of global trials. At the same time, the producers of 'nowheres' in clinical research (*instrumental rationality*) are greedy and sagacious. For they carry their procedures to a growing number of places, filling clinical trials with the features of particular contexts while striving to cover everything with hazy clouds of objectivity.

Once again, it is important to point out that embedding clinical trials in places demands not only a search for 'bodies' and 'patients', as some authors tend to put it. Indeed, previous analyses insisted on describing a trials industry that strives to approach patients and have 'access to their bodies to test new drugs' (Fisher 2009, p. 127); is concerned with 'the scarcity of human subjects'

(Angell 2005, p. 30); fosters 'the competition for access to ... sick bodies' (Shah 2006, p. 158); and tries to 'get bodies into a trial in the first place and to keep them there throughout the life of the experiment' (Epstein 2007, pp. 182–183). The search for biological bodies is indeed going on but this is the clinical part of trials, and not really their sociological dimension. If companies composing the global trials industry can be depicted as 'body hunters' (Shah 2006), they should also be framed as 'context hunters'. For the establishment of trials also asks for adjustments to the features of places and their inhabitants' customs. In this framework, *communication* appears as a pivotal resource to be explored by global actors.

One might argue that the fact that trials are embedded in local contexts (that is, the fact that conducting clinical research depends on specific arrangements and relations at the local level) is not an issue at all, because the trials industry needs only to ensure the comparability of data produced in clinical trials, on the one hand, and the accuracy of the statistical instruments with which those data are analysed, on the other. In this way, the emergence of *mediational action*, which is carried out in medical sites all over the world, would be of relevance for sociologists but completely meaningless from the viewpoint of those who are simply trying to discover new drugs and therapies. To this argument, I would respond with two crucial considerations.

First, without *mediational actions*, clinical studies would be rapidly paralysed because these *actions* can translate the standards of global companies into the everyday language spoken by local actors and research subjects. It was shown that some *spontaneous* local phenomena are clearly acknowledged, and sometimes welcomed and stimulated, by pharma companies or CROs. These global actors are aware of their limits when it comes to dealing with local matters. For instance, their lack of medical expertise obliges them to look for the support from health institutions, so that the dearth of communication between global companies and patients can be coped with. It is then important to ask whether this strategic mediation should really be realized in health institutions, and especially those which are owned by the national state. The trials industry's necessities end up being looked for in hospitals and clinics, many of which have to struggle to fulfil their basic health care duties as a result of poor governmental investments.

Second, there is a hidden issue of intellectual property here. As I argued, clinical trials also derive from creative schemes, solutions and relations that appear at the local level. From the newsletter created by the research coordinator in Porto Alegre, through the screening sessions at the weekend organized by a clinic in London, to the work of nurse-recruiters in Pretoria, several examples can be invoked of local inventions enabling the conduct of global clinical trials. In this way, it is important to ask who is really designing global clinical studies. So far this innovative task has been attributed exclusively to pharma companies and CROs, which are responsible for the initial draft of protocols. A creative role has never been recognized for research sites, investigators, coordinators, nurses and other professionals.

From a political point of view, this state of things is comfortable because it is practical to consider people based in medical settings as mere 'service providers' and pay them a stipend during the conduct of a trial. Equally, it is practical to provide an individual company, which is considered as the clinical study's designer, with a long-lasting patent on the final medicine deriving from a study. However, a clinical trial is much more than the protocol written in a company's office. For one of its most decisive aspects is the choice of tactics and procedures that render the study feasible at the local scale. Thus, if we are really to reward people for their innovative efforts throughout the development of a pharmaceutical product, reserving the trial's prizes for a handful of global companies is an insufficient (and maybe unjust) decision.

When talking about trials embedded in local contexts, I am not referring to a curious, exotic dimension of trials. I am claiming that innovations advanced by *instrumental actors* would be ineffective without the *complementary* and creative role played by *communicational* and particularly *mediational* actors. The trials industry is not simply passing by local contexts and getting rid of these features on completion of its studies. Rather, it is diving deeper and deeper into local contexts in order to have their mistakes repaired and their limitations minimized. The sociological, communicational and mediational dimension of trials can remain hidden, and can therefore be ignored or denied by any sort of analyst. However, it cannot be detached from global trials without the latter being deprived of a pivotal part of themselves.

The geographical dimension of trials goes beyond these issues and reflections. In this chapter, we focused on phenomena happening in urban contexts. Subsequently, we analyse the impacts of global trials for countries and national states.

5

Globalization: Clinical Trials and International Hierarchies

In the first part of this book, the impacts of global standards on the hospitals' structures were analysed. In the previous chapter, a broader approach was introduced, drawing attention to the ways in which the trials industry benefits from the configuration and dynamics of cities. In the present chapter, an even broader perspective will be introduced, focusing on the consequences of global trials for the different countries.

Frequently, the trials industry strives to depict its international studies as examples of humanitarian effort toward the emergence of a better and healthier world. Countless examples have been cited by analysts (Shah 2006; Petryna 2009; Fisher 2009), so let us simply consider that International the Federation of Pharmaceutical Manufacturers and Associations declares that its 'primary role is to improve global health'.[1] On the one hand, the trials industry speaks of an international effort to 'improve global health.' One the other hand, these humanitarian concerns have been stifled by a large set of calculations and economic matters whose effects have been the production and reinforcement of global inequalities. In order to analyse this trend, we shall focus on three issues: the formation of a hierarchy of countries in global trials; the identification of 'productive countries'; and the scheme of competitive recruitment.

5.1 What are Rescue Countries?

The trials industry would always prefer to invest in countries whose past performances serve as a sort of clinical guarantee, enhancing the likeliness of good results and quick procedures. It is largely known that the United States and Western Europe are the world regions in which the trials industry believes

---

1   On the Federation's website: www.ifpma.org.

to be able to make sound and safe investments (Shah 1996; Epstein 2007; Petryna 2009; Fisher 2009). These regions hold large numbers of key opinion leaders.[2] In addition, the initial phases of trials tend to be concentrated in these traditional national settings because these studies generally involve few participants, a characteristic that would render their dislocation to other regions too costly.[3]

As a result of this rationale, a sort of global hierarchy of countries come to be defined, comprising three groups. On the top of the list are the countries that, from the industry's viewpoint, are more experienced and trustable (such as the United States, Germany, the UK, France, Belguim, Spain, Italy, and a few others). At the bottom of the list, there are countries which are seldom or never utilized by the industry. Actually, this is the group involving the largest number of national situations. As I claimed elsewhere (Bicudo 2011), one has to be cautious when talking about 'global' trials because the industry depends, in fact, on a few countries holding the infrastructures and human skills necessary to run its sophisticated studies.

The intermediate group is composed of countries that are slowly attracting the global companies' confidence. Typically, these are countries where the trials industry goes whenever recruitment is difficult in traditional settings. Thus these countries are mobilized in order to 'salvage' studies, and that is why they are frequently touted as 'rescue countries'. Brazil and South Africa are in many instances considered and utilized in this way.[4] Generally speaking, this group of countries have five main characteristics.

First, in the mid-1990s those countries were suddenly bombarded by a plethora of international studies. Their regulatory framework and institutional bodies (such as ethics committees and regulatory agencies) were not prepared to cope with this inflow of studies, being obliged to improvise and adjust as they could (Bicudo 2012). Consequently, their regulatory approval of studies, from the industry's viewpoint, has been slow and cumbersome in comparison with traditional national settings. For example: 'These start-up timelines are two to three months in the United States (US) and approximately four months in the European Union (EU). In Brazil this process can take 6 to 7.5 months...' (Dainesi and Elkis 2007, p. 285).

---

2   On opinion leaders, see section 3.1.
3   In a hospital in Paris, the Director of Projects of a research unit told me that some phase 1 and 2 studies may involve as few as two or three people.
4   Russia, India, China and Mexico would be other examples.

Second, rescue countries generally hold large populations, making a rapid recruitment of participants more likely. The Managing Director of a South-African CRO told me: 'We're all quite quick at putting on patients on a study and we often get the highest numbers.' This is also the portrait drawn in Johannesburg by the Director for Clinical Management of a multinational CRO:

> *We're talking about a population of 45 million [inhabitants]. So we've got an enormous patient population. And in some global studies, the moment we can get approval, we can get all our patients in two weeks, sometimes in a month…*

> **How many patients in two weeks?**

> *The most patients we've got in two weeks is 200. And that is our quota for what we've committed to. We got them all…*

Thus, in a so-called rescue country like South Africa, the trials industry can enjoy the impressive average recruitment of 100 patients in a single week.[5] This is why the Operations Manager of a private research centre in Pretoria is confident to say:

> *South Africa is, I think, traditionally, always a rescue country … They [pharma companies and CROs] open up the Americas, the Western European countries, and if they do not deliver [patients] on time, they always open up South Africa as rescue site. And we always seem to deliver. We can really deliver.*

> **Okay, in spite of this slow regulatory process?**

> *Unfortunately … You know, taking that into consideration, once the study is approved, you know, usually South Africa takes all the patient numbers…*

The same phenomena take place in Brazil. Talking about the choices made by pharma companies and CROs, a Contract Specialist I interviewed in São Paulo declared: 'they are not crazy to close Brazil because Brazil puts a big amount of patients into the study, sometimes in less time than other countries had been given. It loses in the regulatory process but wins in the recruitment.'

---

5   However, recruitment rates always depend on the disease at stake, the period of the year, and other factors.

A third feature of rescue countries is that they may hold large populations of people with a particular disease. The classic example is clinical research on HIV, a domain that has experienced an important expansion since the 1990s (Scrooten et al. 2001). South Africa has become an almost unavoidable setting for HIV trials, due to the large occurrence of the disease.[6] As a Research Coordinator who works for an NGO in Johannesburg told me, HIV in South Africa is frequently associated with tuberculosis, turning the country into a favourable setting for studies on both diseases. According to a CRO's Director for Clinical Management: 'We did a feasibility [study] recently where they asked us for 200 HIV patients and after we've done the feasibility, we got 70,000 patients.'

A fourth characteristic of rescue countries is their ethnic diversity, which according to some authors is an important feature for global researchers (Epstein 2007; Petryna 2009; Marschner 2010). In Pretoria, for example, I visited a private clinical research centre. As the company has access to both rich, white populations and black, poor communities, it can assimilate many types of studies, placing them into different areas depending on the studies' nature. Ethnic diversity is complemented by the economic disparities of these countries, meaning that they hold many sorts of diseases. As the Managing Director of a local Johannesburg CRO told me:

> In South Africa you basically have all the diseases. You've got your emerging world diseases like your TBs [tuberculosis] etcetera but then you've also got your emerged or first world diseases, your schizophrenias, your oncologies, your gastric complaints ... Pretty much you can do any sort of trial in South Africa...

Finally, there is another feature of rescue countries: in some instances, running trials there can prove less costly. Here, it is simply the exchange rates that can do the trick, according to the detailed explanation of a CRO employee who oversees trials conducted in both South Africa and Europe:

> And would you say that running clinical trials in South Africa is less costly compared to the UK?
>
> Yes, I would say so. How it works is, we get given a budget, in pounds, or we get given a budget in dollars, US dollars. And if I get given,

---

6   According to the United Nations, about 17 per cent of the South African population was infected with HIV in 2008.

say, 1,000 dollars for this one procedure and you changed it with our exchange rate ... Now a pound is twelve rand. So they give 1,000 pounds, so it's actually 12,000 rand that I have to negotiate with ... But in South Africa that procedure only costs 2,000 ... So I'm not going to pay them [the investigators] 12,000 if it is only actually 2,000. You see, so we actually do, in some respects, get given a lot more money than is needed, but I don't give all the money to the doctor. I'll say: 'Well, you only need 100 rand, you're only getting 100 rand ... I do trials in Europe and I do in South Africa, and I can see the difference in the budget ... Say, in England it is 18,000 pounds that they get per subject, whereas in South Africa it will be only like 7,000 pounds per subject ... Just because of the exchange rate...

The Managing Director of a South-African CRO claimed: 'Generally, we're about 25 per cent cheaper than Europe and the States'. It is difficult to verify the accuracy of this estimation, as there are many economic factors involved. However, it seems that the difference is not substantial. In 2008, the Tufts Center for the Study of Drug Development compared the costs of drug research in some countries. An index was created, with the United States being given the index 1.00. South Africa was the first country cheaper than the United States (index 0.99), whereas the UK was the first country above the United States (1.09). Arguably, this quite small difference is due to the high number of oncologic trials conducted in South Africa, as the country has to recur to some importations (of laboratory tools and contrasts, for instance) needed in these studies. In addition, countries like South Africa tend to have their costs increased because they receive more international studies. However, in some other countries low costs seem to be an important factor for the trials industry. In the index of the Tufts Center, Brazil, for example, was given the index 0.61, and is therefore significantly less expensive than the United States (1.00).

These five characteristics render the so-called rescue countries strategic settings for phase 2 and 3 studies, in which large populations must be recruited. According to Anvisa, the Brazilian regulatory agency, 80 per cent of the studies conducted in the country in 2010 were developed by multinational companies; of these studies, 63 per cent focused on phase 3 whereas only 4 per cent focused on phase 1; 22 per cent on phase 2; and 11 per cent on phase 4. Therefore, within the *instrumental* strategies of global companies, rescue countries have been given a clear function and area of operation.

However, regardless of the role played by the different countries, they are all led to join an international competition for trials and payments, as we shall see in the next section.

5.2 Criteria to Include or Exclude Countries

Economists talk about opportunity costs: whenever someone invests in an economic factor, costs must be faced which correspond to the advantages of other factors that have been forgone. The smaller the relative productivity and benefit of the chosen factor, the higher its opportunity cost is.

Global companies must also make choices, which frequently implies the selection of the appropriate countries to include in studies. As the choice of a country may imply the exclusion of many others, one could say that each country has its own opportunity cost. That is why CROs must be very careful whenever they spread trials globally. In other words, they have to prefer countries 'that are known for their productivity', as a British President for Clinical Management described it.

Basically, there are three ways in which these geographical choices are made. In the first case, the sponsor (pharma company) indicates the countries to include in the trial. Second, the CRO can take over the responsibility for this choice. Finally, countries and sites can be selected through discussions between the pharma company and the CRO. In all the cases, we are dealing with *instrumental* decisions framing countries as economic opportunities.

At certain moments, certain regions or countries can enjoy especial conditions that make them good trialists. As Petryna (2009) showed, some Eastern European countries such as Poland, the Czech Republic and Bulgaria had become key places to enrol research subjects by the end of the 1990s. This was mainly due to the presence of large populations lacking health care, a quick regulatory process, and a health care staff willing to glean the scientific and economic resources delivered by global trials. At subsequent moments, however, such special conditions may suddenly fade away. A Global Director for Patient Recruitment based in London explained to me that nowadays Eastern Europe's recruitment performance has deteriorated. Among other reasons, this happened due to the integration of this region into the European Union with the consequent unification of timelines and regulatory frameworks. Therefore, the research prosperity and hardship experienced by different countries has been strategically attached to *instrumental* decisions taken by global companies.

From the industry's standpoint, one can point to four factors making countries more or less interesting at certain moments. First, there is a 'population factor', which is the sheer number of inhabitants. Countries with large populations are therefore the most attractive.

The second aspect has a 'monetary' nature and has to do with the costs incurred by the trials industry in each country. As mentioned in the previous section, some institutions have prepared studies comparing national costs, and some professionals seem to be aware of these discrepancies. For instance, the Operations Manager of a private research centre in Pretoria said: 'What is currently happening is, conducting studies in India and in South America and in the Ukraine and Hungary is maybe cheaper than what South Africa is.'

Third, there is a 'legal factor'. The trials industry would prefer to conduct studies in countries whose regulatory framework is in line with its global standards. In the European Union, for example, the publication of the Clinical Trials Directive, in 2001, was intended to unify and speed up national regulatory procedures, making the legal environment more friendly at the global companies' eyes (Boussuge 2004).

Finally, there is an 'infrastructure factor'. Historical processes may lead to the emergence of special medical infrastructures in certain countries, favouring the installation of some types of trials. In Paris, a CRO's Director for Clinical Management told me that oncology has been a burgeoning area of studies in the country: 'in France, we are lucky to have ... anti-cancer centres, which were created by general De Gaule after the [Second World] War, and which are very, very well structured to do clinical research ... There are 20 anti-cancer centres.'

Some factors (legal and infrastructural) can be modified by the national government while others (population and monetary) can only be the object of precarious and limited control. The final combination of factors creates a research atmosphere that is more or less interesting for global companies. Gradually, then, the rise in the number of global trials sparks an international competition for the trials industry's prizes. If these phenomena frequently take a subtle shape, there is a recruitment strategy whose existence has been provoking a clear and open competition between sites and countries, as we see next.

5.3 What is Competitive Recruitment?

As we have seen in the case of rescue countries, the trials industry sometimes wants particular countries with particular features to figure in a trial. However, these concerns are frequently lacking and the main criterion is simply the number of research subjects that can be recruited, as well as the pace of recruitment. Time is as crucial as, or maybe more crucial than, the size of the study population enrolled in each national setting. In order to abet rapid and efficient recruitment schemes, the trials industry has formulated a strategy known as competitive recruitment.

After determining the global n,[7] the company selects a group of countries and sites that could develop that particular trial. No specific number of patients is assigned to each site; therefore, each research team recruits as many subjects as it can. As a consequence, competition begins. The selected research teams must hurry up in order to get regulatory approval and deal with all clinical issues implied by the recruitment. Once the global n is exhausted, the process is terminated. In a study that would require, for instance, 100 patients, one site may end up recruiting 30 participants whereas another one would recruit only 2. According to a British Vice-President for Clinical Management: 'between investigators in the same country you can get very radical differences in how many patients are recruited'.

To be sure, this recruitment scheme stimulates competition between sites and research teams. At the same time, this research staff's work is decisively informed and shaped by the rules and procedures mandated in each country. Teams operating under fast regulatory systems take advantage of the scheme, as they are frequently able to start recruiting before many other teams in many other national settings. Thus it can be claimed that we are also dealing with a competition between countries. Needless to say that rescue countries, with their commonly slow regulatory process, tend to have poorer performances in this international competition. According to a Brazilian Site Identification Manager:

> It may happen that the study proposal is sent to all the [selected] countries, recruitment begins and Brazil is late due to the regulatory process. So countries are recruiting ... The United States opens up sites in three months and is already recruiting. We cannot open up sites in less than seven months and we have to wait four months more to start

---

7   About the n, see section 1.5.

recruiting. So we are really unfavoured by competitive recruitment ...
Then, many times when recruitment is competitive, Latin America is
excluded because the United States has found the patients, Europe has
found the patients, and Latin America closes down.

In South Africa, sites and teams have faced the same frustrations. According
to the Operations Manager of a private research centre in Pretoria, some studies
are lost in which 'the rest of the world has put all the patient numbers because
we did not obtain [regulatory] approval in time'.

As competitive recruitment is used in a growing number of global trials,
these hardships tend to rise. Eventually, the need for efficiency and rapid
processes, which stems from global companies, turns the international scenario
into an arena in which countries fight for payments, patients and studies. Even
in the European Union, where there has been legal harmonization, competition
cannot be completely obviated. For the regulatory assessment of studies must
take 60 days but countries are allowed to mandate shorter delays (Boussuge
2004).

5.4 Clinical Trials and International Hierarchies

The *instrumental rationality* of the global industry cannot help instrumentalizing
whole regions and countries. In spite of its dealing with medical issues and
medical institutions, the trials industry frequently triggers processes and
schemes that may be completely strange to the sphere of medicine. In São
Paulo, the Manager of a private research centre told me that his company is
sometimes offered clinical studies formulated by multinational companies and
designed to be conducted only in Brazil. According to him, this is done because
'they have some drug left'.

> *How does a pharmaceutical company sell its medicines? They don't offer*
> *the drug to pharmacies, they offer it to physicians. It is the physician*
> *that will issue a prescription ... They have to look for physicians so*
> *that the physician gets convinced that the medicine is the best one, it*
> *is good and so on ... So in order for them to accept: 'I'll give you this*
> *medicine for free, within a clinical study, you will become aware that*
> *the drug is really safe and good, and you'll start prescribing it.' So it is*
> *a marketing strategy. So they have some drug left from a clinical study.*
> *The drug expires in two years. 'Are we going to throw it away? Let's*

give it for free, let's create, let's write a rubbish protocol [laughter], and give it to physicians for free so that they can have a first contact with the drug, which will be soon launched into the market and will be bloody expensive...'

Certainly, this description, as well as other similar accounts, may be the product of witticism or exaggeration. In addition, one might argue, bad trials can only be conducted in bad sites. However, this discussion may be of interest for bioethicists and ethics committee members, being much less relevant from a sociological standpoint. When one looks at processes that have undeniably taken place in hospitals, cities and countries, it is easy to realize, on the one hand, that medical research has been permeated by rationales that do not have much to do with the healing purposes of medicine; on the other hand, one perceives regulatory renewals, infrastructural modernizations and partnerships being diligently implemented. Thus, even if global trials are really the realm of benefits and fairness, different local actors seem to have their medical purposes distorted, operating under pressure in order to join competitions and meet targets they have not established themselves. As we shall see in the following chapter, whenever this rush is coupled with the hardships of diseases, the outcome is a situation of intense tension and hopelessness.

6

Hope: The Symbolic Dimension of Global Trials

There must be no fear of delivering a topsy-turvy explanation, as this is precisely the interpretative tactic mandated by a world dominated by paradoxes, inequalities and opposing interests. In this way, it is time to turn our approach upside-down, going back to the realm of *communicational rationality* and focusing on local relations and micro-processes.

The gathering of knowledge of diseases and health, as well as the production of tools and devices to be used in medical settings, are among the most remarkable deeds in human history. They surely belong to the process of 'rationalization' classically described by Max Weber (1979). They are also part of the effort described by Hannah Arendt (1998), through which human beings strive to offset their natural limitations. However, the outcomes of human actions can never be fully controlled.

> *Because the actor always moves among and in relation to other acting beings, he is never merely a 'doer' but always and at the same time a sufferer ... the story that an act starts is composed of its consequent deeds and sufferings (Arendt 1998, p. 190).*

Medical activities can certainly be invoked as an example of this unpredictability of human actions. Instead of representing a peaceful pathway whose final stage would be the complete understanding of health and disease, medical activities frequently reveal human limitations. Throughout the centuries, every new medical success (of which man was certainly a 'doer') was accompanied by a set of gray areas and doubts (which turned man into a mere 'sufferer'). As a result, history seems to bring about waves of hope, insofar as societies are always waiting for brighter times when their present incapacities will supposedly be surmounted by new sets of discoveries and technologies.

Clinical trials reflect these human dilemmas. On the one hand, even the sophisticated medicine of our times fails to provide us with all the answers and devices needed to counter old age, sickness and death. On the other, this very same medicine promises us a bright future, as research and innovation never cease to be undertaken. Eventually, global clinical trials tend to become a sort of 'global machine of hope'.

If, as Santos (2000a) pointed out, the geographical space is composed not only by 'objects' but also by 'actions', it possesses a strong content in terms of expectations, hopes and ideologies. For actions are always informed by cultural and ideological values, as many sociologists have stressed. Thus in the geography of international clinical studies, there is also a symbolic dimension.

In order to analyse these processes and their impact on local actors, research sites and countries, I shall comment on five phenomena. First, I revisit explanations stressing the symbolic dimension of medicines. Then, we look at trials by considering diseases that are barely understood by physicians and scientists. We move on to analysing the role played by trust and hope in clinical trials. After looking at the institutional fragilities of hospitals, clinics and regulatory agencies, I finish the chapter by focusing on the ever-growing need for clinical studies.

6.1 The 'Symbolic Efficacy' of Medicines

A global clinical study generally implies the provision of medications or devices. In some cases, patients of state hospitals can even access technologies that are not provided by the state.[1] What is more, news about a clinical study can sound particularly appealing when people consider that the access to medications will be costless. According to Timmermans and Berg (2003, p. 72), clinical studies 'are sometimes primarily a means to obtain drugs free of charge (in the case of industry-subsidized trials, for example)....'

To be sure, these phenomena have their limitations. Even though the use of placebo (and especially pure placebo[2]) has been decreasing compared to what

---

1   For example, on the issue of pharmacological stents in cardiologic trials, see section 3.5.
2   Nowadays, in many trials participants receive the standard-of-art drug *plus* placebo, whereas other participants would receive the same state-of-the-art drug *plus* the candidate drug. Pure placebo occurs when state-of-the-art therapy is withdrawn and subjects may end up receiving only the placebo. This type of trial tends to be quickly rejected by most ethics committees if detailed and convincing justification is not presented.

happened in past decades, in some trials subjects may be given an ineffective candidate medicine. However, it is important to recall that in *communicational rationality*'s realm, we are no longer concerned with *therapy* (that is, the solution of medical problems from a scientific point of view); when one focuses on the issue of *care* (that is, the situation in which someone is looked after[3]), even the provision of a placebo can signal a caring attitude, enhancing the feeling of trust and hope experienced by those who face a disease and undergo medical treatments. (By the way, the fact that providing medicines and pills can signal the caregivers' *caring* attitude helps us to see that *communication* takes place not only by means of words but also through flows of objects endowed with social meaning.)

As Van der Geest and colleagues (1996, p. 167) remind us: 'Efficacy is brought about in a context of belief and expectation and through social communication and interaction.' In other words, medicines and treatments, in addition to their scientific dimensions, also hold decisive cultural and symbolic meanings (Etkin 1988; Benoist 1989; Lefèvre 1991; Van der Geest et al. 1996). From the point of view of *communicative actions*, the actual scientific efficacy of medicines can be less important than their 'symbolic efficacy', to use the classic expression forged by Lévi-Strauss (1996). However, *instrumental actors* can also use these psychosocial aspects of medicines for their own benefit. For example, as Abraham (2007, p. 44) claims: 'It is much more important to the pharmaceutical manufacturers that their products are *regarded as effective* by regulators, the medical profession and (increasingly) by patients, *than whether they really are effective*.'

In phase 4 trials, the symbolic dimension of research is enhanced because the drugs studied are already available on the market, having shown some satisfactory results in the past. As a member of a London research team explained to me, somebody who joins a phase 4 study may be provided with a medication that he or she has already taken in the past, as part of normal treatment. Phase 4 trials are proliferating not only because of the trials industry's willingness to further assess its drugs but also because some physicians can select medicines and propose investigator-initiated studies.[4] In Madrid, I visited a private clinical trials centre created by physicians based in different hospitals. Of the seven trials initiated by this group in 2010, four were investigator-initiated studies. As phase 4 trials become more frequent, scientific and economic interests, on the one hand, and the symbolic dimension of therapies, on the other, tend to form strong blends.

---

3   On the conceptual distinction between *therapy* and *care*, see section 3.6.
4   We focused on these studies before, but from a different point of view, in section 3.5.

Therefore, the symbolic efficacy of medicines can manifest itself also in clinical trials. First, its emergence has to do with the normal attitude of human beings faced by diseases and treatments: the attention that is delivered contains a *caring* meaning. Second, this symbolic dimension is enhanced, in advanced phases of trials (such as phases 3 and 4) because of good (and maybe outstanding) results obtained in previous phases. Thus, even if people are given placebos in a trial, these therapeutically ineffective pills may still be endowed with a symbolic efficacy. As we will see, the communicative aspects of medicines and investigations can be further accentuated by the intrinsic limitations of medicine.

6.2 The Limits of Medicine

As we have seen,[5] some physicians may stress the medical potentialities of clinical trials, an attitude that is also related to the limitations experienced by certain medical specialties. Rose (1985, p. 34) provides us with an example:

> *Most non-infectious diseases are still of largely unknown cause. If you take a textbook of medicine and look at the list of contents you will still find, despite all our aetiological research, that most are still of basically unknown aetiology.*

Indeed, it is only by talking to physicians that one begins to realize that the lack of effective therapies is more frequent than one might suppose. Challenged by the hardships imposed by some illnesses, both physicians and patients may end up framing participation in clinical trials as an unavoidable *tactic*. In Paris, for instance, a neurologist spoke of the relative easiness with which people can be put into neurological studies: 'I think that it is a domain which is not very complicated [in terms of recruitment] because there are not many therapies.'

Furthermore, in certain medical domains, physicians and patients can only rely on therapies whose efficacy is known to be limited. In fields such as oncology or tuberculosis, diseases can display a resistance that compromises the performance of medicines. In this way, a clinical trial may turn into a medical scapegoat for desperate patients who have tried various and ineffective treatments.

---

5   Chapter 3.

These issues are frequently ignored by CROs. From their vantage point, the physicians' recruitment performances are commonly attributed to their sites' organization and infrastructure. CROs pay little attention to the fact that these performances may have to do with the sufferings imposed by the disease under study, as a paediatrician explained to me in Paris:

> *'There are indeed some doctors who recruit much more quickly than others ... The doctor I am thinking about treats very young children who are 2, 3, 4 or 5 years old and have dramatic rheumatic diseases. These are children who suffer all the day long. Okay? And it is evident that their parents look for an intervention that can relieve the child. Then, as soon as they are proposed a study that might improve the situation, everybody says yes...*

In this way, a good recruiter is not only the physician-investigator who relies on appropriate infrastructures and teams but perhaps also the one whose medical specialty is laden with sufferings and therapeutic pressures. As a French neurologist put it, the key issue 'is not only the physician's effectiveness; it is also the patient's expectations'.

To summarize, there are some domains in which therapeutic discoveries have been scant. In these areas, clinical trials can be marshalled in an attempt to realize, via candidate medicines, what standard therapies fail to deliver. As a consequence, and from the point of view of *mediational* and *communicational* actors, there is a content of trust and hope in clinical trials, as we shall see in the following sections.

6.3 How Trustable are Clinical Trials?

In all the five countries I studied, physicians were asked the following question, providing me with approximately the same answer given by a French physician:

> **Does the public generally have good knowledge of clinical trials in France? Do people know what trials are about?**

> *No. They make mistakes, they believe they are guinea-pigs, they think that ... They have a quite mistaken notion.*

In the opinion of this French investigator, as well as his colleagues in France and other countries, recruiting subjects would be simpler without this widespread, unclear view of trials. Some people claim that the media further complicates the situation because global trials 'don't have a good press' as a CRO's Director for Site Management put it.

Although it is hard to assess the accuracy of my interviewees' pessimistic view, it seems that for many people, participation in trials is automatically associated with the image of 'guinea pigs'. When the trials industry and caregivers need to find subjects for a trial, it is within this negative cultural framework that they have to operate. However, if, on the one hand, clinical trials can be framed as an uncertain or even dangerous activity, they are, on the other hand, salvaged by the presence of a medical staff that conducts the study's procedures. Indeed, caregivers are often inspiring trust and 'forging convictions' (Scott et al. 2011). Their 'interactional involvement' with patients has an important 'potential to influence the decisions of patients to enrol, or not to enrol, in clinical trials' (Mueller 2004, p. 43).

Beyond all the technicalities and standards of trials, the actual recruitment depends, to a large extent, on personal relations between caregivers and potential research subjects. Frequently, as a Research Coordinator based in a hospital in Madrid said, recruitment happens through 'a conversation between the physician and the patient'. We are dealing with a situation in which *validity* is the main rule. For the investigator and the patient have to come to a state of *intercomprehension*. According to a co-investigator who works in a hospital in Paris: 'a patient takes the decision [regarding participation in a trial], evidently, by considering his or her troubles and fears but the major factor is the relation to the physician and the trust toward the physician'.

A Spanish rheumatologist explained that good relations with patients can generate good recruitment performances:

Are there doctors who are faster at recruiting participants?

Yes, because it depends on the capacity to convince or the established relation between the doctor and the patient. Our patients are chronically sick for the most part, so it is relatively simple for us, when we propose them to take part in a clinical trial ... We seldom have difficulties because the patients already know us. There are doctors who need to have a good relation to patients. And it is simpler for these doctors to recruit.

Oh, so rapidity depends also ...

It depends on the relation and the capacity to inspire confidence in the patient.

Because the patient becomes more trustful ...

The patient becomes more trustful and if the doctor says that something has to be done, the patient does it without any concern.

According to a cardiologist interviewed in São Paulo, experienced physicians acquire a sort of medical intuition that is put into practice when it comes to recruiting research subjects:

> *The physician, due to his experience with research, knows how to approach patients, according to the patient's profile ... For instance, we are the hypertension group. So all the physicians who work here are dedicated to arterial hypertension ... So the physicians know how the patient's profile is, how the patient likes being looked after. When they are searching for cases for a study, they already know how to approach patients.*

This same cardiologist acknowledges that nowadays, the health system is becoming the main target of the patients' hopes, as physicians are losing the 'aura' they used to be invested with. Indeed, as Salter (2001, p. 881) claimed, we have witnessed the slow degradation of the 'societal respect for the authority of the users and dispensers of medical knowledge'. Nevertheless, the fact that trials are conducted in medical institutions still seems to provide patients with some guarantees. As a CRO's Clinical Manager based in Madrid claimed, the recruitment of participants is facilitated by the patients' trustful stance toward the Spanish health system. In Porto Alegre, another cardiologist voiced an interesting argument:

> **What are the patients' motivations to accept to participate [in trials]?**

> *I think, in the first place, it is the empathy toward the hospital and the service of the hospital ... Patients trust the hospital very much ... So they believe in the physicians no matter who the physician is. They know that if they are here they will have a good service, both in terms of technology and human resources...*

Thus, even though the physician has become a less central player, respect toward the medical institution can be decisive in the recruitment of research subjects. In fact, the trust in medical settings can offset the anticipation of risks in clinical trials. Hospitals are places where debilitated people look for help and assistance; in this context, it is difficult to completely prevent the emergence of feelings, affects and emotions, factors that can shape the ways in which people make risk assessments (Slovic 1999; Finucane et al. 2000). In a medical environment, where care is provided, people would therefore feel more protected when joining potentially harmful studies.

As noted in the previous section, physicians' recruitment performances have to do not only with technical factors. By looking at actual relations in concrete sites, it is easy to realize that some *communicational* events must also be in place in order for trials to be conducted efficiently. Thus clinical research is not only the realm of *facticity* (elements that determine precise ways of acting) but also the realm of *validity* (wayward relations in concrete contexts). In order to have a true comprehensive perspective, more than a technical and biological approach, a cultural and sociological approach is needed.

In this way, it is important to trumpet the misleading nature of some individualistic (or psychic) approaches. For example, three psychiatrists (Appelbaum, Roth and Lidz 1982), after studying the situation of participants in two psychiatric trials, proposed the idea of 'therapeutic misconception', referring to the fact that research subjects can misunderstand their participation, framing it as therapy rather than research. The idea of 'therapeutic misconception' has been adopted by many bioethicists and even some sociologists (Schaeffer et al. 1996; Lidz and Appelbaum 2002; Kimmelman 2007; Madsen, Holm et al. 2007). In the framework of the theory of communicative action, this idea of therapeutic misconception amounts to 'sociological misconception', for it falsely suggests that *communicational actors* could eventually adopt the mental framework of *instrumental actors*, thereby correcting their 'misconceptions'. As this putative correction does not take place, analysts tend to attribute some type of psychic disturbance or limitation to research subjects. This interpretative tendency is unavoidable, as in the founding article of the idea, it is said that among the research subjects studied, schizophrenics proved very likely to treasure their caregivers and express misconceptions.

> It is possible that chronic schizophrenics, with their severe cognitive impairment, and borderlines, with their tendency for magical thinking and overvaluation of their care-takers, are particularly susceptible to the therapeutic misconception (Appelbaum, Roth and Lidz 1982, p. 329).

Certainly, a physician might deceive people by making them believe that in a clinical trial, therapeutic purposes prevail. However, even in this situation there is no misconception, from a sociological point of view. For both actors (the physician and the patient) would be sharing the *background knowledge* that a physician is supposed to look after people, even if this is done by the indirect means of a clinical trial. If patients join a study in order to solve their personal medical problems, it is necessary to distort the interpretation in order to speak of misconception, insofar as clinical trials are always proposed by caregivers in medical settings, and not by managers in private companies' offices or by scientists in mesmerizing laboratories. In this sense, it does not seem helpful to talk about 'procedural misconception' either, pointing out that in clinical research, 'human subjects are cast or cast themselves into the roles of patients rather than research subjects or participants' (Fisher 2006, p. 265 note 6). If people decide to play the roles of patients in hospitals and in their relations to caregivers, then this attitude proves that they hold a good conception, rather than a misconception, about medical institutions.

To a large extent, these distorted interpretations are provoked by partial views, through which analysts ignore the communicative contents of trials, such as the presence of trustful relations. Parallel to the occurrence of trust, global trials can awake a whole set of hopes.

6.4 Global Trials for Hopeful Patients

As I claim throughout this book, clinical trials can be seen from two different points of view or, more precisely, in the light of two *rationalities*. This coexistence of rationales in the domain of medicines was perceived before, although in a different theoretical framework, by Van der Geest and collaborators (1996, p. 170):

> *Pharmaceuticals constitute a perfect opportunity for the study of the relation between symbols and political economy. On the one hand, they are a part of the international flow of capital and commerce. On the other, they are symbols of hope and healing and of the promise of advanced technology.*

The 'promises' of clinical trials can be very telling at the local scale, especially for patients facing resistant or intense pain and hardships. At those moments, hope is a key factor leading to participation in research, as explained by the director of the research unit of a London hospital:

> *Where you've got a sort of illness like migraine, because it is so unpleasant, people are much more willing to be involved in research because they can see or they hope there will be a potential positive outcome for them, whereas if it is something like high blood pressure, most patients find that the treatment that you give them is worse than having high blood pressure...*

In this sense, the *mediational action* plays another crucial role by canalizing the patients' hopes. At the outset of a medical treatment, hope is always involved, because the erratic development of diseases obviates certainty about improvement. Whenever the treatments adopted by caregivers fail, patients' hopes can be transferred from established medicines to the candidate drugs tested in clinical trials. Even though this shift leads to greater uncertainties and risks, they can be alleviated by the presence of the medical staff that proposes and conducts the study, mediating between global companies and research subjects. From this point of view, *mediational actors* really have to speak the *communicational* language. For it seems that patients would never accept participation if a socially shared knowledge (a background knowledge) was lacking: the assumption that the medical responsibilities of caregivers toward patients are always present, even in research contexts.

Timmermans and Berg (2003, p. 71) also highlighted the relevance of hope in clinical trials:

> *Patients bring their own goals and hopes to the research protocol. Viewed from the trajectory of patients, a protocol ... is a source of hope, often the only perceived means to combat the disease that has stricken them ... They rarely care about the research goals of the protocol (although sometimes they do); all they care about is preserving life and having a possible future.*

The interference of hope is another factor expanding the leeway for *validity* in trials. For the passage from normal treatment to a clinical study must be agreed upon by patients and caregivers. Here, however, there is no leeway for the emergence of the *conspiratorial* agreements made between trials companies and some physician-investigators. Here, *intercomprehension* and negotiations take place in *explicit* ways, as the passage from normal treatment towards a trial happens in the context of a medical *institution*, in which physicians never lose their primary responsibilities as caregivers. Even though the participants' hopes can be spoiled by the study's implications, and turned into frustration, at the stage focused on in this book (that is, the initial stages of trials), hope is at its utmost force and does play a decisive role.

Not surprisingly, then, patients can establish quite big commitments when they are proposed participation. In some instances, the anticipation of benefits seems to overrule important difficulties. In a clinic in London, for instance, some people travel long distances and come from other British cities in order to undergo the study's procedures and receive medication. Although such displacements are quite rare, there are certainly small 'research migratory flows' in several countries. This shows that the failures and limits of medicine may be enhancing some people's hopes. Nevertheless, in addition to these symbolic factors, there are also key institutional fragilities to be foreground in our analysis.

6.5 Global Trials for Hopeless Hospitals

In an interview in Johannesburg, the Research Coordinator of a NGO gave me an answer that has become commonplace in the universe of trials:

> *In your opinion, what are the reasons for people to participate in clinical studies?*
>
> *[Deep breath.] One of the reasons is because the public health system is inefficient. So, for instance, for our study, they come to the clinic, they get assessed and they do more regular assessments than they would get in the public hospital. And they come, we do it quickly for them, they don't have to sit there the whole day ... If they have other issues that come up, that need medical attention, we also attend to those, even if it is outside what we are researching.*

The fact that people feel to receive more medical attention in trials was noted by Mattson and collaborators (1985), as well as in Fisher's (2009, pp. 136–137) study on clinical trials in the United States: 'patient-subjects explicitly compare their experiences in drug studies to standard medical care and find that they receive more "care" in clinical trials'. Fisher explains that this feeling is motivated by some circumstances: subjects have more contact with nurses and physicians in trials; they spend less time waiting to be seen; they undergo more examinations more frequently, enabling the diagnostic of parallel diseases. Thus research subjects perceive that they have much medical assistance in a trial and 'often discuss this reason as one on which they would base their recommendation of clinical trials to others' (Fisher 2009, p. 138).

The same impression seems to take place in the countries I visited. As we have seen,[6] patients frequently volunteer for trials and indicate studies to relatives and friends. Thus, as claimed in the first part of this book, clinical trials have been normalized into the medical *reality* of many institutions.

In pressing contexts, clinical studies may be regarded as a very reasonable medical option. This same interviewee (the South-African Research Coordinator of an NGO that runs clinical trials on HIV and tuberculosis), told me that some years ago, patients used to be recruited from six different state clinics located in a poor suburb of Johannesburg. After a while, the nurses of this NGO could simply stop visiting clinics because patients began to be referred to the research unit spontaneously. Thus, when a new patient goes to the clinic, he or she is immediately sent to the NGO in order to try to join a clinical trial. Those clinics, probably facing difficulties at coping with the big inflow of sick people, have incorporated clinical trials into their medical routines and started referring people to clinical research even without being asked to do so.

These considerations have become particularly important after a global trend toward the reduction of the national state's power. Even in those countries with a strong health care system (such as the UK, France and Spain), where the state used to play important steering roles as well as provide high-level services, this medical excellence has been jeopardized over the last years. Consequently, clinical trials end up being perceived, by both physicians and patients, as 'better than standard medical care' (Fisher 2009, p. 137). For instance, in the UK, as a consequence of macroeconomic austerity measures, more and more services tend to be removed from the scope of the NHS,[7] which seems to be destined to be slowly dismantled. A physician who is based in London considers that hospital administrators may now feel forced to privilege industrial trials:

> *Hospitals just need more research income, so they switch from investigator-initiated trials to pharmaceutical-sponsored trials. Because*

---

6   Chapter 4.
7   The UK's national health system.

[pharmaceutical companies] pay better and investigator-initiated trials are always underpaid somehow because they are always struggling for money. So what we see is that it is harder to get our investigator-initiated trials into the system because if there is a competing industry-sponsored trial, the hospital will always go for the industry-sponsored trial, 'cause it pays better.

The dearth of therapies, which is typical in some fields of medicine, tends to be coupled with a dearth of institutional weight and state control. In this way, doctors and administrators have been abandoned to their medical fate in hospitals that sometimes lack basic tools and structures. Not surprisingly, some physicians, after being proposed a study from the trials industry, may become quite enthusiastic, a feeling that leads to suitable recruitment performances for CROs and pharma companies.

The trend may be further reinforced by the procedures of regulatory agencies, some of which are faster at allowing the initiation of trials than registering drugs approved in clinical studies. In this way, the allowance of experimentation ends up being easier than the register of therapies, and the whole pharmaceutical system becomes biased towards experimentation. Associated, all these phenomena increase the global need for global trials.

6.6 The Symbolic Dimension of Global Trials

Instrumental actors have difficulties to embed their actions into specific contexts. This is not the case in the universe of *communicational rationality*, in which actions are always referred to concrete needs and products. Here, all beliefs and decisions are informed by shared values that, although precariously acknowledged by those who hold them, are surely effective and strong.

The world as the sum total of possible facts is constituted only for an interpreter community whose members engage ... in processes of reaching understanding with one another about things in the world. 'Real' is what can be represented in true statements, whereas 'true' can be explained in turn by reference to the claim one person raises before others by asserting a proposition (Habermas 1996, p. 14).

For global, *instrumental actors*, the main concern is the production of 'true things' by means of discursive and intellectual instruments such as statistical tools. On the other hand, *communicative actors* create, and are informed by, 'real things' insofar as their actions are oriented towards a range of shared objects, knowledge and values. It is in order to understand the production of 'real things' (of *reality*) within clinical research that is important to analyse the ways in which global trials are reshaping the organization and structure of hospitals.

To cope with its lack of medical expertise, the trials industry needs to engage in partnerships with caregivers based in hospitals. These relationships are nowadays considered as natural and obvious, especially by those who are used to matters of clinical research. However, from a communicative standpoint, it is precisely the easiness, obviousness and triviality of this scheme (in a word, its *reality*) that needs to be discussed and problematized.[8]

At first sight, it can appear natural that clinical studies conceived and sponsored by the trials industry are undertaken in hospitals and other medical practices. However, the accustomed eyes that many people turn to this phenomenon may be disregarding crucial issues and pressing problems. It is only by analysing the details of global trials that one can understand how international clinical research is shaping the *reality* of hospitals and clinics.

In research sites, pressing problems must be coped with. Confronted by diseases and impending deaths, *mediational actors* must struggle with all the means available. The limitations of medicines, the hopes of patients, the institutional weaknesses of hospitals, and the procedures of regulatory agencies help form a context in which clinical research tends to become a mandatory activity. As Timmermans and Berg (2003, p. 80) noted, for some patients 'the offer of a last try might be too hard to resist'. Thanks to their limitations and pressures, caregivers can also frame clinical trials as a 'last try'.

At this moment, the paradoxes of clinical research, which reflect the paradoxes of our times, display their dramatic face. On the one hand, *mediational actors* have learnt to use the *instruments* proposed by global companies, putting them at the patients' disposal. In a Spanish oncologist's words: 'our goal as physicians is try to help the patient to get better in the cancer. That means that the patient is not a means to know the compound, but the compound is a means to heal the patient.' On the other hand, however, the power of multinational

---

8   By the way, there are many 'natural' phenomena in clinical trials which might be subjected to critical views. For instance, people tend to normalize the fact that one physician, having recruited 50 patients for a trial, will receive a larger payment than another physician who has enrolled 5 subjects. Is it really correct to consider that the former investigator's clinical work is more valuable than the latter's?

companies, as well as the *conspiratorial* agreements of world trials,[9] creates several types of fragilities and dependencies, as the account of a Research Coordinator based in Porto Alegre reveals:

> *One of the worst things is the person who goes into the study and doesn't want to leave it. The person doesn't manage to break the linkage. That happens, you know. So we have to make it very clear: 'Look, if the study doesn't work, you'll have to go back to your original physician…' And many of them don't want to.*

> *They don't want to because of…*

> *Because of care…*

The proliferation of global trials may imply the rise in the population (of patients, physicians and sites) that becomes unable to 'break the linkage' to international research, especially if it is hoped that these relations will help solve medical limitations. To be sure, the conversion of global trials into a global machine of hope is an almost unavoidable effect. The phenomenon is indeed at the root of a society whose technological progresses never cease to make promises. What is regrettable, however, is that this machine is turning into a model of health care for patients who would otherwise depend on hospitals and clinics whose vitality fades away in a more or less rapid manner. As a physician told me in London: 'it is always better for the patient to be in the trial than not being in the trial. It offers them more than standard medicine would, in any case.'

It is important to stress this natural way in which many people tend to frame the association between hospitals and trials. Repeating the discourse of many physicians in all the countries I studied, a doctor based in Madrid claimed: 'We consider that, in general, clinical trials are the best treatment because they offer you the possibility of giving a plus, something else, in comparison to conventional treatment.' Another physician, based in Paris, declared: 'if I were a patient, I would wish to be in a clinical trial because I know that patients of clinical trials are looked for very, very well.' After listening to similar claims countless times, it is unavoidable to think that for some physicians, traditional health care tends to be seen as a second-hand alternative whereas clinical trials would be the 'gold standard' of medicine. Fisher (2009, pp. 136–138) noted that some patients consider clinical research as 'higher-quality care'. As clinical

---

9   On the idea of *conspiracy*, see the first part of this book.

trials penetrate deeper into hospitals' structures, this view tends to be adopted by some physicians as well.

Moreover, the line separating clinical research and medical care may be blurred by some patients' or physicians' attitudes. For instance, my fieldwork revealed several situations in which patients looked for hospitals not to have access to health care but as prospective research subjects.[10] This is the account provided by one physician-investigator in São Paulo, somebody who works in a state-academic hospital and also runs a private practice:

> In my private practice, I do general infectology. I have many patients with hepatitis C and many patients with Aids. Rich patients of my private practice tell me: 'Look, if there is a study with a new medicine for hepatitis C, I want to volunteer, okay?' ... As they know that we are doctors based in universities, they tell us: 'Look, if you get a study, I want to be a guinea pig,' it is the word they use [laughter]. 'I want to be a guinea pig because I need new treatments' ... I don't need to mention anything, I don't need to propose anything...

So the 'guinea pig', from a terrible situation that had to be avoided by any means, is gradually turning into a medical target. Many similar examples could be invoked in order to advance that, more and more frequently, there seems to be people who, under the pressure of diseases, seem to prefer to be seen not by a physician but by a physician-investigator. In countries where health care systems work precariously or have been dismantled, the trend can be stronger, because people have learnt that in a global study, procedures are undertaken according to international, high-quality standards.

Slowly, a new *reality* emerges. On the one hand, the trials industry, physicians and administrators, through various *implicit* agreements, provide hospitals with new technical, human and administrative resources, which are informed by the global companies' demands. On the other hand, health care is gradually associated with, or even replaced by, research activities. As a result, old frontiers become fluid or disappear altogether, favouring the emergence of a new *reality* that is subjected to the industry's managing power. Subsequently, this reshaped *reality* will be the basis for the formulation of new global standards on clinical research. *Realization* and *standardization* become, therefore, endless and *complementary* processes.

---

10   On this issue, see Chapter 4.

These tendencies cross over the fragile borders of research sites, imposing even more pressing challenges to national governments in the grips of recessions, fragilities and hard international negotiations. Hit by the waves of economic crises (in the UK, Spain or France), or fighting the inheritances of their shaky historical formation (in Brazil or South Africa), national states may feel tempted to also deposit their hopes into the hands of the trials industry. As London and Kimmelman (2008, p. 83) pointed out, welcoming global clinical studies may represent 'the desperation of host communities'.

Perhaps, the biggest reason for concern, when it comes to global trials, is the 'overneed' experienced by *communicational* and *mediational* actors, at the local level. As the world population of research subjects increases, *communicational densities* turn recruitment and participation into key demands. Eventually, we would be witnesses to the formation of a desperate crowd, which needs trials for gaining monetary reimbursements; trials for compensating for the medicine's incapacities or the doctors' negligence; trials for enjoying the confidence deriving from warm and close *health care*; trials for offsetting failures of various therapeutic lines; trials for escaping the frailties of agonizing state hospitals; trials for the trials' sake, why not, because, let's reflect, dangerous and deleterious activities would never be allowed into the solid and communitarian premises of medical institutions.

These growing needs are quickly identified and captured by the trials industry, which can then spread the image of heroic multinational companies whose operations would be filling the gaps left by fragile national health systems. This discourse, insofar as it refers to concrete needs experienced in concrete places, acquires an apparent legitimacy and helps to hide series of technical calculations and *implicit* schemes that have little to do with actual medical concerns. In this way, 'structures of undamaged intersubjectivity found in nondistorted communication' (Habermas 1996, p. 148) are constantly kept at bay. If national states continue to be deaf to the needs voiced at the periphery of the political system, mystifications and distorted discourses will be the prevailing phenomena in global trials, impairing the consolidation of *democratic* schemes, *explicit* agreements and clear *communication*.

Conclusion

Intermediary Groups and Sociology

The issue of *mediation* is very old in the history of social sciences. The topic acquired its force with Marx, whose classic analysis of commodity unravelled the economic mediations between the capitalistic and the working classes. In addition to these fundamental classes, Marx pointed to the presence of an intermediate group of small producers. Even though Marx's basic assumption was the slow disappearance of intermediate groups, some analysts following his tradition have been responsible for further explorations on the subject.

For instance, Poulantzas (1974) identified the emergence of a 'non-monopolistic capital' mediating between the 'monopolistic capital' and the 'small capital'. The main trait of this intermediary group would be its extreme dependence upon the standards enforced by the monopolistic capital. Olin Wright (1989), wishing to highlight the concept of exploitation, formulated an explanation in which intermediary classes are seen as social groups being exploited in some dimensions of social life but promoting exploitations in other dimensions. Jean Lojkine (1981) spoke of 'intermediary social layers' which realize a twofold and ambiguous move, displaying both traits of ascension and decadence. Milton Santos (1979), after describing two basic 'economic circuits', pointed to the presence of an intermediary circuit, called 'marginal superior', which displays some features of both basic circuits. Here, I mention only these four classic interpretations insofar as they share some theoretical characteristics with the analysis proposed in this book.

Even though I do not address the issue of social classes, I certainly draw attention to social mediations. Within the framework of the theory of *communicative action*, mediation is a decisive phenomenon, as no real *communication* can happen without the presence of some kinds of *mediational* resources. Among these resources, language can be seen as a fundamental one and can be said to possess a material dimension. Before Habermas, the objective, material nature of language had been grasped by Sartre (1960, p. 180): 'Word is material. In its appearance (an appearance that, as such, is endowed with truth), the word strikes me materially like the movement of the air that produces some reactions in my organism...'

Thus previous sociological and philosophical interpretations acknowledged both the presence of *mediation* between social groups and the role of *communication* as a basic *social mediator*. In this book, however, I strove to highlight two phenomena that have received little attention.

First, intermediary social groups are worth noting not only because they happen to fall between two other groups of social actors but also, and especially, because they enable the *dialogue* (albeit indirect) between the society's poles. Thus, more than speaking of an intermediary group, I am talking about the existence of a *mediational action*. This mediating role tends to become more and more decisive in our contemporary society, as a result of two concomitant processes. On the one hand, specialized groups (like scientists) are constantly sophisticating their specialized *codes*, therefore undermining the possibilities of a direct *communication* with laypeople. On the other hand, the reiterated crises and limits of capitalism oblige global companies to anchor their operations into local contexts, in order to minimize the abstract character of their operations. In this way, the mediational action turns into a major social pillar, forestalling processes of drastic social disintegration.

Second, I tried to show that in our contemporary society, *social mediation* requires much more than the use of tools and relations that would be *spontaneously* picked up in the social environment. In order for *mediational actions* to emerge and consolidate, it is necessary to marshal various instruments, institutions and professionals.

We can summarize the basic features of *mediational action* as it emerges in global clinical trials:

- It captures the main components of local contexts, making them less piecemeal and therefore more controllable from the point of view of instrumental actors;

- It grasps and solidifies the fluid communicational densities, putting them at the global actors' disposal;

- It translates the global companies' standards into a medical language, enabling clinical trials to be framed as healing activities;

- It corrects the frailties and inconsistencies of global strategies, which can be manifested as soon as instrumental actors install their activities into local contexts;

- It helps to minimize the risky appearance of clinical studies, through the trustable presence of caregivers;

- By taking place in concrete locations, it provides local actors with a geographical reference, defining settings they can go to in order to have access to global instruments;

- It submits local actors to new timelines, through the social diffusion of efficient schemes and rigid deadlines;

- It collects the instruments of global actors and places them at the local actors' disposal, enabling the alleviation of some immediate needs;

- It enhances and multiplies the content of hope in clinical trials, by covering technical activities with the hues of health care;

- It helps to multiply some needs lurking at the local scale, through the translation of everyday troubles into a medical language.

Habermas (1981, 1996) spoke not only of *actions* but also of *rationalities*, referring to particular logics with which social actors organize relations and products. It is important to stress that the emergence of the *mediational action* does not lead to the appearance of a new rationality. *Mediational actors* are always striving to adjust and speak either the language of *instrumental rationality* or that of *communicational rationality*. However, they are unable to formulate a language of their own. This limitation is primarily due to the configuration of capitalism, which continues to be underpinned by only two basic principles: the logic of capital and the logic of work, as explained by Marx (1990).

Arguably, *mediational actions* manifest themselves not only in the domain of global clinical trials. It would be possible to indicate three examples where the same phenomenon comes into play. First, local companies have been performing a mediating role in translating the standards of global mobile phone companies, thus enabling an astonishing diffusion of this technology. Second, wholesalers and other local companies specialized in logistics have permitted a successful distribution of food and drinks produced by global companies. Third, local companies are translating global formulas into national idioms in order to enable the installation of standardized television shows that are turning into globalized products of entertainment. In all these cases, we are dealing with actions taking place at the local scale and facilitating the arrival of the *instrumental rationality* of multinational actors. Thus the occurrence of *mediational actions* opens up promising fields for sociological inquiry in this era of advanced globalization.

Towards a General Theory of Communicative Action

Habermas performed an invaluable work by establishing the foundations of a *theory of communicative action*. However, it seems that all the potentialities of his theory have not been fully explored, which is due to two factors. On the one hand, the thorough exploration of the theory requires the identification of meaningful empirical topics of study, a task that is not always clear-cut in our contemporary, paradoxical world. One the other hand, Habermas himself lost track of his theory's itineraries because he was unable to dispose of old theoretical aspects that barely fit the *communicative* approach. For example, his insistence on the distinction between 'public' and 'private' turns into an awkward element. As Arendt (1998) demonstrated, this distinction, from a sociological perspective, is devoid of meaning. For we are now dealing with societies in which private matters have emerged in the public realm, completely blurring the old distinction.

Moreover, the full exploration of Habermas' theory demands the formulation of further conceptual elements fostering its force without compromising its useful simplicity. It seems to me that the main advancement to be made is the move from the idea of 'action' towards 'systems of actions', an expression proposed by Santos (2000a). Indeed, certain modalities of action become independent from their original authors, coming to be normalized and integrated into the features of groups and places. They begin to impose functions, expectations and behaviours to the members of social groups. In this way, more than speaking of *communicative action*, it becomes necessary to focus on *systems of communicative actions*. This shift would help us understand that *communication* depends not only on human actors but also, and increasingly, on material and technical structures whose absence interrupts the flows of communication.

The study of *systems of communicative actions* would enable us to erase the last traits of individualistic approach present in Habermas' theory. Freed from these elements, the theory would fully open its communicative and counterintuitive wings, thus becoming capable of more promising sociological flights. It would then be possible to move from a 'special' towards a 'general theory of communicative action.'[1] Moreover, it would be possible to get rid of heavy concerns about coherence, and to focus on the meaningful paradoxes of contemporary societies.

Global Trials and Institutionalization

In 2010, the UK's government launched a policy that, albeit controversial, is likely to be followed by other countries. Clinical researchers, whether they are based in the academia or pharma companies, can send proposals to have access to clinical data kept in state hospitals. This includes information such as types of prescriptions, occurrence of illnesses, registries of rare diseases, lifestyle information, among others. In 2013, one of the directors of the Medical Research Council defined the policy as follows: 'The Government hopes that by enabling safe access to NHS patient records for research, the UK will be a more attractive place for the pharmaceutical industry to do research, which will create jobs and boost the UK economy'.[2]

The programme, which rapidly attracted the industry's interest[3], was denounced by some actors and groups as a threat to patients' confidentiality. However, there have been few analysts focusing on its political implications. It is known that the international pharmaceutical production system has been failing to guarantee broad access to medicines and therapies. Therefore, it seems insufficient to enable the conduct of more and more clinical protocols and the arrival of more and more medicines to the market. In addition, if the

---

1 This terminology is inspired by Albert Einstein, the physicist who proposed a 'general theory of relativity' as an expansion of his own 'special theory of relativity'.
2 Dr Janet Valentine, head of Public Health and Ageing (http://www.insight.mrc.ac.uk/2013/09/03/qa-research-using-patient-data/).
3 From January to December 2012, the industry submitted 41 proposals to have access to clinical information. In addition, it funded 13 investigators based in universities. Therefore, of 166 submissions received in the period, the industry participated in 54, which amounts to 32.5 per cent (Isac 2012, p. 15).

government becomes more flexible and generous when dealing with its clinical data, it is worth wondering whether the industry will also soften some of its core policies in terms of intellectual property, prices, information sharing, definition of research pathways and so on.

To governments and laypeople across the world, it is important to know whether global clinical trials can contribute to the construction and consolidation of *democratic* societies. This adjective has to be used in a sparing way because of the strong and diverse meanings it carries. In the framework of a *communicative* interpretation, *democratic* schemes will be guaranteed whenever relevant issues raised at the periphery of the political system (in the citizens' everyday life) can be *communicated* throughout the system, reaching the 'parliamentary complex' (institutions and spheres of state) (Habermas 1996). In this sense, the examples reviewed in this book bring about serious doubts about the *democratic* contents of the relations between the trials industry and some clinical investigators. To a large extent, companies and investigators are free to make decisive choices that escape the steering control of medical *institutions*.

To be sure, important differences exist between the five countries studied. In the UK the *institutionalization* of trials has attained an interesting level. In most British hospitals, clinical trials can be subjected to a set of scientific assessments and economic management that restrain the investigators' arbitrariness. In its turn, South Africa seems to have a long walk to go in its search for control over the arrangements made by global companies and investigators. Interestingly, it is the only country in my 'sample' where private hospitals and practices can equal, and sometimes outpace, the relevance of state research sites. Especially in studies such as oncologic ones, which have displayed a steady expansion in the country, private sites are of paramount relevance. As these sites tend to be less bound to strictly abide by rules of public accountability, the South African scenario of clinical research remains decisively shaped by *implicit* negotiations and source agreements of precarious clarity. The danger, here, is that physician-investigators may favour their role as investigators and economic actors, framing their basic and *explicit* medical responsibilities as ancillary elements. Spain and France are moving toward the UK's situation, whereas Brazil is clearly struggling to rub out the traits of old epochs when the *institutionalization* of trials was scarce and weak.

Regardless of the country's particularities, clinical trials are still a domain in which *validity* and *implicit* negotiations find much leeway to emerge. This situation will persist as long as the initial steps of studies continue to strongly depend on the decisions taken by individual investigators and companies (source agreements). In all these countries, the preoccupation voiced in Porto Alegre by a Research Coordinator based in a state hospital can be echoed:

> We want CROs or sponsors to stop calling me or someone else or whatever to say: 'Do you want to participate?' And I agree and register ... We want the representative of the institution [hospital] to receive the proposal ... There will be criteria to distribute the work.

In all the countries studied, therefore, *explicit* decisions tend to be jeopardized by a plethora of schemes escaping the control of institutions and state agencies. Moreover, it is worth considering that regulatory and sanitary agencies of several countries continue to depend, to a greater or lesser degree, on fees received from the trials industry. This circumstance limits their independence and willingness to forestall political abuses (Abraham 2009).

However, it is possible to admit that this state of things is not the final configuration of global trials. Much can still be done in order to enhance the role of *institutions* and legitimate law. As Habermas (1996, p. 384) claimed, the state is always

> a delicate and sensitive – above all fallible and revisable – enterprise, whose purpose is to realize the system of rights anew in changing circumstances, that is, to interpret the system of rights better, to institutionalize it more appropriately, and to draw out its contents more radically.

If, on the one hand, clinical trials have imparted much power to global companies, they also constitute, on the other hand, an opportunity for physicians to perform their *explicit* tasks of caregivers and enhance their capacity to take medical decisions. Furthermore, this role played by physicians has enabled the access of local actors to the *instruments* of global companies, allowing local *tactics* to extract some force from the features of global *strategies*. Thus the *communicative* dimension of global trials (which is only realizable when one pays attention to relations and creations existing at the local scale) proposes some clues to policy-makers and analysts concerned with the elaboration of more *democratic*, and therefore less *conspiratorial*, social arrangements.

To a great extent, policy-makers and national governments would already glean interesting political results if they were able to observe and foster some positive creations and arrangements already established in global trials. The instrument of research contracts, the coordinating role played by Research Foundations and the presence, in hospitals, of collective boards to assess the need for new clinical studies are examples of *institutional* mechanisms that can be beneficially explored in national policies. Therefore, many programmes and initiatives can be launched to explore the medical potentialities of trials, taming (or at least minimizing) the weight of particularistic and financial impulses.

What seems to complicate things is the paradoxical nature of the *mediational action*. Even in those cases in which physicians and caregivers do adopt more collective and *communicative* stances, they never cease to be interested actors who may be seduced by the trials industry. Actually, the *instrumental* and *communicational* rationalities are always present and *entangled* within the mediational action. By joining a global trial to protect the patients' well-being in the first place, a physician is, at the same time, facilitating the trials industry's global *strategies* and realizing source agreements that defy the steering role of local institutions. There is no conceptual separation. In other words, Schrödinger's cat is always there, inside the box, dead *and* alive at the same time.

Such impasses do not have to instil in us any type of political desperation. Increasing the steering force of *institutions* and streamlining the legal environment of global trials will also imply the enlargement of global companies' fields of choices. However, there is no reason to consider that the trials industry and the state are deadly enemies lacking any type of common purpose. Acting wisely, the national state can canalize the industry's ambitions so that *instruments* can be put at the patients' disposal in politically beneficial and careful ways. In addition, the business strategies of companies can be allowed to carry on insofar as they do not spoil either the financial soundness of the state or the medical vitality of hospitals and clinics.

Nowadays, global trials have already been integrated into the *reality* of hospitals, being part of the physicians' and patients' sets of needs. Fighting against global companies would simply amount to a huge loss of energy. With political sagacity and theoretical seriousness, policies can certainly be conceived at the local and national scale, so that the enterprise can be informed by *explicit* rules of *institutions* and the binding force of legitimate law.

To be sure, the formulation of such policies will depend on the particular features of each country. However, one can suppose that, everywhere, one of the most effective tactics to be mobilized by governments and policy-makers is the exploration of contextual and local aspects of global trials. Possibly, beneficial effects will be triggered once the activity is connected to local aspects, needs and creations, becoming less dependent on global standards. In this way, *mediational actors* would be eventually incited to admit that the *instrumental rationality* provides them with a fundamental working language, but the *communicational rationality* is, and will always be, their legitimate native tongue.

Bibliography

Abadie, R. (2010) *The Professional Guinea Pig: Big Pharma and the Risky World of Human Subjects*. Durham, NC, Duke University Press.

Abraham, J. (1993) Scientific standards and institutional interests: carcinogenic risk assessment of benoxaprofen in the UK and United States. *Social Studies of Science*, 23, 3, 387–444.

Abraham, J. (2007) Drug trials and evidence bases in international regulatory context. *BioSocieties*, 2, 41–56.

Abraham, J. (2009) Sociology of pharmaceuticals development and regulation: a realistic empirical research programme, in S.J. William, J. Gabe and P. Davis (eds), *Pharmaceuticals and Society: Critical Discourses and Debates*. Oxford and Malden, MA, Wiley-Blackwell, 54–66.

Almeida, E. and Bicudo, E. (2010) Psicoesfera e medicina: meio construído urbano e congressos médicos na América Latina. *Revista Geográfica Venezolana*, 51, 2, 179–201.

Angell, M. (1997) The ethics of clinical research in the Third World. *New England Journal of Medicine*, 337, 12, 847–849.

Angell, M. (2005) *The Truth About the Drug Companies: How they Deceive Us and What to do About It*. New York, Random House.

Appelbaum, P.S., Roth, L.H. and Lidz, C. (1982) The therapeutic misconception: informed consent in psychiatric research. *International Journal of Law and Psychiatry*, 5, 3–4, 319–329.

Arendt, H. (1998) *The Human Condition*. Chicago, IL, University of Chicago Press.

Beck, U. (2005) *The Risk Society: Towards a New Modernity*. London, Sage.

Benner, P.E. (1989) *The Primacy of Caring: Stress and Coping in Health and Illness*. Wokingham, MA, Addison-Wesley.

Benoist, J. (1989) Le médicament, opérateur technique et médiateur symbolique. *Projections: la santé au futur*, 1, 45–50.

Bicudo, E. (2006) *O circuito superior marginal: produção de medicamentos e o território brasileiro*. Master's Degree Dissertation. Department of Geography, University of São Paulo.

Bicudo, E. (2011) 'Geographical randomization' and 'social exploitation' in clinical research: world trials in Santiago, Chile. *Health and Place*, 17, 807–813.

Bicudo, E. (2012) *Globalization and Ideology: Ethics Committees and World Clinical Trials in South Africa and Brazil*. Ph.D. thesis. Department of Poltical Economy, King's College London.

Bourdieu, P. (1989) *O poder simbólico*. Lisboa, Difel.

Boussuge, J. (2004) *Transposition en droit français de la Directive Européenne 2001/20/CE: nouvelle procédure d'autorisation des essais cliniques et enjeux associés*. Ph.D. thesis. Faculty of Pharmaceutical and Biological Sciences, University Paris V (René Descartes).

Busfield, J. (2006). Pills, power, people: sociological understandings of the pharmaceutical industry. *Sociology – the Journal of the British Sociological Association*, 40, 2, 297–314.

Chow, S.-C. (2011) *Controversial Statistical Issues in Clinical Trials*. New York, CRC.

D'Enfert, J., Lassale, C., Prod'homme, P. (2003) Attractiveness of France for clinical trials: assessment by pharmaceutical sponsors. *Thérapie*, 58, 3, 283–289.

Dainesi, S.M. and Elkis, H. (2007) Current clinical research environment: focus on psychiatry. *Revista Brasileira de Psiquiatria*, 29, 3, 283–290.

Durkheim, É. (1932) *De la division du travail social*. Paris, Félix Alcan.

Epstein, S. (1996) *Impure Science: AIDS, Activism, and the Politics of Knowledge*. Berkeley, CA, University of California Press.

Epstein, S. (2007) *Inclusion: the Politics of Difference in Medical Research*. Chicago, IL, University of Chicago Press.

Espeland, W.N. and Stevens, M.L. (1998) Commensuration as a social process. *Annual Review of Sociology*, 24, 313–343.

Etkin, N. (1988) Cultural constructions of efficacy, in S. Van Der Geest and S.R. Whyte (eds), *The Context of Medicines in Developing Countries: Studies in Pharmaceutical Anthropology*. Dordrecht, Kluwer, 299–326.

Finucane, M.L., Alhakami, A. Slovic, P. and Johnson, S.M. (2000) The affect heuristic in judgments of risks and benefits. *Journal of Behavioral Decision Making*, 13, 1, 1–17.

Fisher, J.A. (2006) Procedural misconceptions and informed consent: insights from empirical research on the clinical trials industry. *Kennedy Institute of Ethics Journal*, 16, 3, 251–268.

Fisher, J.A. (2009) *Medical Research for Hire: The Political Economy of Pharmaceutical Clinical Trials*. New Brunswick, NJ and London, Rutgers University Press.

Foucault, M. (1999) *Surveiller et punir: naissance de la prison*. Paris, Galimard.

Foucault, M. (1988) *Naissance de la clinique*. Paris, Presses Universitaires de France.

Fox, R.E.C. (1998) *Experiment Perilous: Physicians and Patients Facing the Unknown.* New Brunswick, NJ, Transaction Publishers.

Gadow, S. (1985) Nurse and patient: the caring relationship, in A.H. Bishop and J.R. Scudder (eds), *Caring, Curing, Coping: Nurse, Physician, Patient Relationships.* Montgomery, AL, University of Alabama Press, pp. 34–37.

Gilligan, C. (1982) *In a Different Voice: Psychological Theory and Women's Development.* Cambridge, MA, Harvard University Press.

Gray, B.H. (1975) *Human Subjects in Medical Experimentation.* New York, John Wiley and Sons.

Habermas, J. (1987) *The Theory of Communicative Action, Vol. 2, Lifeworld and System.* Cambridge, Polity.

Habermas, J. (1996) *Between Facts and Norms: Contributions to a Discourse Theory of Law and Democracy.* Cambridge, MA, MIT Press.

Habermas, J. (2008) *Between Naturalism and Religion.* Cambridge, Polity.

Huntington, S.P. (1952) The marasmus of the ICC: the commission, the railroads, and the public interest. *The Yale Law Journal*, 61, 467–509.

Jonas, H. (1969) Philosophical reflections on experimenting with human subjects. *Daedalus*, 98, 219–247.

Kalt, J.P. and Zupan, M.A. (1990) The apparent ideological behaviour of legislators: testing for principal-agent slack in political institutions. *Journal of Law and Economics*, 33, 103–131.

Keynes, J.M. (2007) *The General Theory of Employment, Interest and Money.* London, Macmillan.

Kimmelman, J. (2007). The therapeutic misconception at 25 – treatment, research, and confusion. *Hastings Center Report*, 37, 36–42.

Kohlen, H. (2009) *Conflicts of Care: Hospital Ethics Committees in the USA and Germany.* Frankfurt and New York, Campus Verlag.

Laffont, J.-J. and Tirole, J. (1991) The politics of government decision-making: a theory of regulatory capture. *The Quarterly Journal of Economics*, 106, 1089–1127.

Lakoff, A. (2005) *Pharmaceutical Reason: Knowledge and Value in Global Psychiatry.* Cambridge, UK and New York, Cambridge University Press.

Lakoff, A. (2007) The right patients for the drug: managing the placebo effect in antidepressant trials. *BioSocieties*, 2, 57–71.

Lantrès, O. (2007) Cohérences et divergences dans la transposition en droit français de la directive 'Essais cliniques', in A. Laude and B. Tabuteau, *Essais cliniques, quels risques?* Paris, Presses Universitaires de France, 37–53.

Lefèvre, F. (1991) *O medicamento como mercadoria simbólica.* São Paulo, Cortez.

Lévi-Strauss, C. (1996) *Anthropologie structurale.* Paris, Plon.

Levine, M.E. and Forrence, J.L. (1990) Regulatory capture, public interest, and the public agenda: toward a synthesis. *Journal of Law, Economics & Organization*, 6, 167–198.

Lidz, C.W. and Appelbaum, P.S. (2002) The therapeutic misconception – problems and solutions. *Medical Care*, 40, 9, 55–63.

Lojkine, J. (1981) *O Estado capitalista e a questão urbana*. São Paulo, Martins Fontes.

London, A.J. and Kimmelman, J. (2008) Justice in translation: from bench to bedside in the developing world. *Lancet*, 372, 9632, 82–85.

Luhmann, N. (1983) *Sociologia do direito I*. Rio de Janeiro, Tempo Brasileiro.

Madsen, S.M., Holm, S. and Riis, P. (2007) Attitudes towards clinical research among cancer trial participants and non-participants: an interview study using a grounded theory approach. *Journal of Medical Ethics*, 33, 4, 234–240.

Marchal, F. (2007) *Processus de gestion des essais cliniques à l'agence française de sécurité sanitaire des produits de santé*. Ph.D. thesis. Faculty of Pharmaceutical and Biological Sciences, University Paris 5 (René Descartes).

Marks, H.M. (1997) *The Progress of Experiment: Science and Therapeutic Reform in the United States, 1900–1990*. Cambridge, Cambridge University Press.

Marschner, I.C. (2010) Regional differences in multinational clinical trials: anticipating chance variation. *Clinical Trials*, 7, 2, 147–156.

Marx, K. (1990) *Capital: A Critique of Political Economy*. London, Penguin.

Mattson, M.E., Curb, J.D. Mcardle, R. (1985) Participation in a clinical trial: the patients point of view. *Controlled Clinical Trials*, 6, 2, 156–167.

McGoey, L. and Jackson, E. (2009) Seroxat and the suppression of clinical trial data: regulatory failure and the uses of legal ambiguity. *Journal of Medical Ethics*, 35, 2, 107–112.

Mirowski, P. and Van Horn, R. (2005) The contract research organization and the commercialization of scientific research. *Social Studies of Science*, 35, 503–548.

Mueller, M.-R. (1997) Science versus care: physicians, nurses, and the dilemma of clinical research, in M.A. Elston, *The Sociology of Medical Science & Technology*. Oxford, Blackwell, 57–78.

Mueller, M.R. (2004) Involvement and (potential) influence of care providers in the enlistment phase of the informed consent process: The case of AIDS clinical trials. *Nursing Ethics*, 11, 1, 42–52.

Noddings, N. (1984) *Caring, a Feminine Approach to Ethics and Moral Education*. Berkeley, CA, University of California Press.

Nowotny, H., Scott, P. and Gibbons, M. (2007) *Re-thinking Science: Knowledge and the Public in an Age of Uncertainty*. Oxford, Blackwell.

Oliveira, R.V.F. (1999) *A rodada do Uruguai e suas implicações para a indústria brasileira: o caso dos direitos de propriedade intelectual na indústria farmacêutica*. Master's Degree Dissertation. Insitute of Economy, University of Campinas (Unicamp).

Petryna, A. (2002) *Life Exposed: Biological Citizens after Chernobyl*. Princeton, NJ, Princeton University Press.

Petryna, A. (2005) Ethical variability: drug development and globalizing clinical trials. *American Ethnologist*, 32, 2, 183–197.

Petryna, A. (2009) *When Experiments Travel: Clinical Trials and the Global Search for Human Subjects*. Princeton, NJ, and Oxford, Princeton University Press.

Piachaud, B.S. (2002) Outsourcing in the pharmaceutical process: an examination of the CRO experience. *Technovation*, 22, 81–90.

Polanyi, K. (1944) *The Great Transformation*. New York, Farrar & Rinehart.

Porter, T.M. (1992) Quantification and the accounting ideal in science. *Social Studies of Science*, 22, 4, 633–652.

Poulantzas, N. (1974) *Les classes sociales dans le capitalisme aujourd'hui*. Paris, Seuil.

Rose, G. (1985) Sick individuals and sick populations. *International Journal of Epidemiology*, 14, 32–31.

Rozovsky, F. and Adams, R.K. (2003) *Clinical Trials and Human Research*. San Francisco, CA, Jossey-Bass.

Sackett, D.L., Oxman, A.D. and PLC, H. (2003) Harlot plc: an amalgamation of the world's two oldest professions. *British Medical Journal*, 327, 7429, 1442–1445.

Salter, B. (2001) Who rules? The new politics of medical regulation. *Social Science and Medicine*, 52, 6, 871–883.

Santos, M. (1979) *The Shared Space: The Two Circuits of the Urban Economy in Underdeveloped Countries*. London, Methuen.

Santos, M. (2000a) *La nature de l'espace: technique et temps, raison et émotion*. Paris, L'Harmattan.

Santos, M. (2000b) *A natureza do espaço: técnica e tempo, razão e emoção*. São Paulo, Edusp.

Sartre, J.-P. (1960) *Critique de la raison dialectique, tome I: théorie des ensembles politiques*. Paris, Gallimard.

Schaeffer, M.H., Krantz, D.S., Wichman, A., Masur, H., Reed, E. and Vinicky, J.K. (1996) The impact of disease severity on the informed consent process in clinical research. *American Journal of Medicine*, 100, 3, 261–268.

Scott, C., Walker, J. White, P. and Lewith, G. (2011) Forging convictions: the effects of active participation in a clinical trial. *Social Science & Medicine*, 72, 12, 2041–2048.

Scrooten, W., Borchert, M., Baratta, C., Smets, E., Kosmidis, J., Goebel, F.D., Wilkins, E.G., Colebunders, R. and The Eurosupport Group (2001) Participants in HIV clinical trials in Europe. *International Journal of STD & Aids*, 12, 94–99.

Serrano, M.A. and Grau, C. (2006) Los CEIC: el dictamen en los ensayos unicéntricos y multicéntricos y los aspectos económicos de los ensayos clínicos, in J. Sánchez-Caro and F. Abellán (eds), *Ensayos clínicos en España: aspectos científicos, bioéticos y jurídicos*. Granada, Comares, 137–156.

Seruga, B., Hertz, P.C., Le, L.W. and Tannock, I.F. (2010) Global drug development in cancer: a cross-sectional study of clinical trial registries. *Annals of Oncology*, 21, 4, 895–900.

Shah, S. (2006) *The Body Hunters: Testing New Drugs on the World's Poorest Patients*. New York, and London, New Press.

Shuchman, M. (2007) Commercializing clinical trials – risks and benefits of the CRO boom. *New England Journal of Medicine*, 357, 14, 1365–1368.

Silveira, M.L. (1996) *Um país, uma região: fim de século e modernidades na Argentina*. São Paulo, Fapesp/Laboplan.

Simmel, G. (1997) *The Philosophy of Money*. London, Routledge.

Sismondo, S. (2009) Ghosts in the machine: publication planning in the medical sciences. *Social Studies of Science*, 39, 2, 171–198.

Slovic, P. (1999) Trust, emotion, sex, politics, and science: surveying the risk-assessment battlefield. *Risk Analysis*, 19, 4, 689–701.

Stigler, G.J. (1971) The theory of economic regulation. *The Bell Journal of Economics and Management Science*, 2, 3–21.

Timmermans, S. and Berg, M. (2003) *The Gold Standard: the Challenge of Evidence-based Medicine and Standardization in Health Care*. Philadelphia, PA, Temple University Press.

Timmermans, S. and Epstein, S. (2010) A world of standards but not a standard world: toward a sociology of standards and standardization. *Annual Review of Sociology*, 36, 69–89.

Tronto, J.C. (1993) *Moral Boundaries: A Political Argument for an Ethic of Care*. London, Routledge.

Turner, E.H., Matthews, A.M., Linardatos, E., Tell, R.A. and Rosenthal, R. (2008) Selective publication of antidepressant trials and its influence on apparent efficacy. *New England Journal of Medicine*, 358, 3, 252–260.

Vallejo, J.M.R. (2006) Normas de buena práctica clínica en los ensayos clínicos, in J. Sánchez-Caro and F. Abellán (eds), *Ensayos clínicos en España: aspectos científicos, bioéticos y jurídicos*. Granada, Comares, 181–201.

Van Der Geest, S., Whyte, S.R. and Hardon, A. (1996) The anthropology of pharmaceuticals: a biographical approach. *American Review of Anthropology*, 25, 153–178.

VOI Consulting (2009) *The Case for Globalization: Ethical and Business Considerations in Clinical Research*. Washington, DC: VOI Consulting.

Wainwright, S.P., Williams, C., Michael, M., Farsides, B. and Cribb, A. (2006) From bench to bedside? Biomedical scientists' expectations of stem cell science as a future therapy for diabetes. *Social Science and Medicine*, 63, 8, 2052–2064.

Weber, M. (1979) *Economy and Society: An Outline of Interpretive Sociology*. Berkeley, CA and London, University of California Press.

Will, C. and Moreira, T. (2010) Introduction – medical proofs, social experiments: clinical trials in shifting contexts, in C. Will and T. Moreira (eds), *Medical Proofs, Social Experiments: Clinical Trials in Shifting Contexts*. Farnham, Ashgate, 1–13.

Wright, E.O. (1989) *The Debate on Classes*. London, Verso.

Index

For Product Safety Concerns and Information please contact our EU
representative GPSR@taylorandfrancis.com Taylor & Francis Verlag GmbH,
Kaufingerstraße 24, 80331 München, Germany

Printed and bound by CPI Group (UK) Ltd, Croydon, CR0 4YY
01/05/2025
01858368-0003